DIGITAL FINANCE

DIGITAL FINANCE

*Security Tokens and Unlocking the
Real Potential of Blockchain*

Baxter Hines

WILEY

Published by John Wiley & Sons, Inc., Hoboken, New Jersey.
Published simultaneously in Canada.

For general information on our other products and services or for technical support, please contact our Customer Care Department within the United States at (800) 762–2974, outside the United States at (317) 572–3993, or fax (317) 572–4002.

Wiley publishes in a variety of print and electronic formats and by print-on-demand. Some material included with standard print versions of this book may not be included in e-books or in print-on-demand. If this book refers to media such as a CD or DVD that is not included in the version you purchased, you may download this material at http://booksupport.wiley.com. For more information about Wiley products, visit www.wiley.com.

Library of Congress Cataloging-in-Publication Data is available:

ISBN 9781119756309 (Hardcover)
ISBN 9781119756323 (ePDF)
ISBN 9781119756316 (ePub)
Interior illustrations created and rendered by Jade Myers

Cover Design: Wiley
Cover Image: © Shutter2U/Getty Images

Printed in the United States of America.

SKY10021815_102120

For my parents, Anne and Bob Hines

CONTENTS

PART III REALIZING THE POTENTIAL OF SECURITY TOKENS

DISCLAIMER NOTICE:

Please note that the information contained within this document can be relied on for educational and informational purposes only. The content, data, and analysis contained herein are provided as they are and without warranty of any kind, either expressed or implied.

This book is not intended as a substitute for the advice of a licensed legal or financial professionals. Readers acknowledge that the author is not engaged in the rendering of legal, financial, technical, or other professional advice. Consult a licensed professional before attempting any techniques or investment in any vehicle discussed in this book.

Past recommendations and investment results are not a guarantee of future results. Using any graph, chart, formula, or other device to assist in deciding which securities to trade or when to trade them presents many difficulties and their effectiveness has significant limitations, including that prior patterns may not repeat themselves continuously or on any particular occasion. In addition, market participants using such devices can impact the market in a way that changes the effectiveness of such device.

Although the author and publisher have made every effort to ensure that the information in this book was correct at press time, the author and publisher do not assume and hereby disclaim any liability to any party for any loss, damage, or disruption caused by errors or omissions, whether such errors or omissions result from negligence, accident, or any other cause. In reading this document, one agrees that under no circumstances are the author or anyone affiliated with the author to be held responsible for any losses, direct or indirect, that may be incurred as a result of the information contained in this book. This includes, and is not limited to, errors, omissions, or inaccuracies.

ACKNOWLEDGMENTS

The genesis of this book came from my deep belief that digital technologies and the blockchain will profoundly impact the financial industry. My experiences in financial technology, research, and investments led me to conclude that a truly revolutionary event was unfolding and its repercussions would have impacts lasting many years into the future. I knew the changes that would eventually come about were multifaceted, complex, and would require the participation of many outstanding people, organizations, and companies. As a result, I would have to draw not only from my own personal experience but also from the guidance and assistance of others to compile what was necessary to make this project a success. The entirety of this work has truly been a team effort.

Throughout my career, I have been very fortunate to have had numerous teachers and mentors who played an important role in my development and intellectual nurturing. The following people will always have a special place in my memory: Frederick Dixon (Portland, Oregon), who gave me my first job in the industry; Leighton Huske (Richmond, Virginia), who took me under his wing during my time with Branch Cabell; Sanford Leeds (Austin, Texas) and Britt Harris (Austin, Texas), who both helped guide me through business school; and Paul Magnuson (Dallas, Texas), whose passion for value investing made a lasting impression on both me and my career.

From my earliest days, family has been my foundation. My sister, Hedley, and brother, Whitfield, have provided love and support throughout the many years. Shirley was always there to lend a helping hand. My wife, Michele, is still with me through all the ups and downs while simultaneously serving as a wonderful mother and friend. My children, Christian and Thomas, have kept me feeling young as I have just crossed over my 40th birthday. My beloved dogs, Brogan and Sydney, in their own magical way never failed to provide comfort and companionship whenever I needed the encouragement to just keep on keeping on.

To my dear friends, Dave Beran and Paul Bullock, thank you for your continued support and faith in me. Your encouragement, advice, and contributions were pivotal in making this book a success. *The two stood by me during every struggle and success along this journey. That is true friendship.*

Thanks to all my colleagues at Honeycomb Digital Investments for all your manifold contributions. I am grateful too to the organizations that accepted my requests for permissions to use their works and to those persons who had the faith and commitment to endorse this book. I would also like to thank Bill Heyn and Brian Bares for providing guidance on key issues along the way.

All of the folks at John Wiley & Sons have been a joy to work with! I want to especially give my regards to Bill Falloon for trusting me to write a book on such a new, complex, and ever-changing topic. From Day 1, I knew deep down that Wiley was the publisher for this work. I was incredibly excited when I learned of Bill's support and his commitment to getting this project off the ground. I am also appreciative for Bill's referral of Jade Myers. The illustrations, graphics, and charts Jade put together were first class and really helped to bring across key points. A special thanks should also go out to editors, Purvi Patel and Samantha Enders, for all of their hard work and efforts in keeping everything moving along.

One last note of appreciation to anyone who has said "You have to read this book!" to a friend or colleague. Those small words make a huge difference in making the time spent writing this book well worth it!

PREFACE

This is an incredibly exciting moment to be involved in finance. There are more and more signs that digitization will transform the traditional investment business model that exists today into a more modern, fair, transparent, and distributed marketplace. This new paradigm will connect investors directly with opportunities via blockchain-based platforms. Just recently, the first regulated security tokens have gone to market. Regulatory certainty has begun to arrive and technology is matching what is needed for this digital future.

Given the significance of this moment, I took a step back to take stock in how I personally got to where I am. My investment background comes from a deeply conservative point of view. During the first portion of my career, I worked in analyst positions at a conventional brokerage house and then at a retirement system for public school teachers. Afterwards, I spent over a decade as a portfolio manager at a firm whose discipline was always to buy blue-chip dividend-paying stocks. So at first, the idea of "crypto" assets and blockchain tokens seemed foreign and frankly, outright crazy. After first hearing about Bitcoin in early 2011, I cannot recall whether I thought it was a scam or a fad – but I likely thought it was both! Like so many others, I was not on the ground floor of Ethereum or any of the Alt-coins. Despite all this, I found myself fascinated with the technology underlying these new manias and how innovative people continued to take it to another level.

After adopting a much deeper understanding of how the technology works and what it could do, I came to realize the blockchain was so much more than simply Bitcoin – and that blockchain technology was not simply going away. It was clear to me that this technological revolution was only going to get bigger and eventually play a major role in the future of the economy, and finance in particular.

Since its origins in 2009, blockchain technology has been somewhat of a rollercoaster. It is important to recognize, though, that this next step of tokenization is not scary, but rather a process with enormous benefits.

In writing this book, I have kept three major points in mind that I feel will help others come to that realization:

First, we tend not to see the forest for the trees when it comes to this emerging space. Everyone has heard about some problem that has come about since the advent of blockchain: the hacking of Mt. Gox and the subsequent theft of millions of dollars of Bitcoins, the role of cryptocurrency in the drug trade that functioned over the website Silk Road, or the use of cryptocurrencies to prop up dictators in North Korea or Venezuela, to name a few. It would be unwise, however, to allow these headline-grabbing occurrences to warp our view of the broader picture.

Throughout history, mishaps and unfortunate events tend to happen when new frontiers open up in the world of finance. We're all familiar with the stories of how Willie Sutton, Bonnie and Clyde, or "Public Enemy #1" John Dillinger terrified the country, targeting insecure banks with their robbing sprees. It actually wasn't too long ago when no one in his or her right mind would have given out a credit card number over the internet to make a purchase. I could go on and on listing similar examples from the past.

Many issues affecting blockchain are getting sorted out as the technology matures, just as would be the case in any emerging technology or advancement. As higher standards are applied and as the market embraces regulatory compliance, so too will the public begin to embrace and trust blockchain. There is no doubt that our current financial system is anything but perfect. Name-brand banks are constantly in the news due to involvement in money-laundering scandals. Financial services firms are frequently bested by cybercriminals who hack user information. The last time I checked, the paper dollars and euros in our system are used in the trade of all kinds of illicit activities! In other words, let's not lose perspective, focus on a few bad apples, and forget all the positive attributes and additions to the financial infrastructure which blockchain technology will provide.

Second, blockchain's complexities cause many to give up in trying to wrap their minds around its many facets. They throw the whole concept into the same category as "rocket science" and are waiting for a more concise explanation of how it works. Albert Einstein said, "Everything should be made as simple as possible, but not simpler" and that "If you can't explain something simply, you don't understand it well enough." My goal in writing this book is to help boil the key concepts down to the essentials and not get bogged down in the details.

Third, people become discouraged when they hear that the once-promised "next big thing" in blockchain gets leap frogged by the "new, next big thing." The pace of development is incredible with almost daily stories of exciting, breakthrough improvements. Some of the best minds from both Wall Street and Silicon Valley are now focused on making the most out of this new technology and the opportunities it presents. That is one thing that won't change.

I'll be the first to tell you I don't have a crystal ball. It is difficult to keep up with the ever-changing environment of technology, cost, and regulation in this market. If I had tried to write out a game-plan predicting how this industry would unfold, then this book would be out of date before its publication.

Instead, my objective is to provide a framework for the potential of what blockchain and security tokens can do within the financial industry. It also will give the reader an understanding of what factors and attributes to look for in determining which projects are most likely to thrive in this new environment.

It seems inevitable that one day all investable assets will be tokenized and that we will see an unbelievable amount of wealth transferred onto the blockchain. There will likely be a time when security tokens are globally traded, and in theory, anyone who has an internet connection and is within the regulatory limits will be able to access and exchange them. This will result in capital market access being democratized, not only for large institutions or the wealthiest classes, but for any investor around the world. One of the most exciting parts about all of this is that everyone can get involved!

Baxter Hines
April 2020

INTRODUCTION

- Blockchain will spearhead the next generation of financial market infrastructure.
- Security tokens are a digitized form of traditional ownership certificates.
- Blockchain and security tokens will disrupt the investment industry by providing cheaper and faster financial market solutions.

Opening Remarks – The Big Picture

Our financial system is on the verge of a massive transformation. The current infrastructure involves complex webs of services, exchanges, and institutions intended to provide an efficient, steady linkage between market participants. Under today's regime, centralization has been the most effective way to trust that all transactions – and the system as a whole – will function reliably and properly. Large organizations, whether they be central banks, multinational brokerage houses, or other financial intermediaries, control the gateways through which money flows around the world; society allows this because these firms have the size, brands, products, and personnel we deem trustworthy. But there is a heavy toll exacted in exchange for a thin veil of confidence afforded by these old-school methods of accounting and verification. This approach is bloated and bogged down by antiquated designs, inadequate integration, bureaucratic stall, and the human tendency to stick with the familiar. The architecture is inadequate for today's needs and inhibits the optimal functioning of a modern globalized economy. A major overhaul to improve efficiencies and drive down costs is long overdue.

Blockchain technology is the solution to spearhead the next generation of financial market infrastructure. Blockchain solves the problem of how to transfer value and information without having to rely on a single thirdparty. Blockchain uses mathematical laws, accounting principles, and governance mechanisms to ensure trust and transparency unparalleled to what our current systems provide today. Cryptocurrencies like Bitcoin introduced the world to blockchain technology and showed how it has the potential to create a reliable, immutable, and auditable system of payments that do not require intermediaries. Cryptocurrency was just the first step and paved the way for the upcoming digital transformation.

1

Security tokens are the next milestone for the financial markets. In simple terms, security tokens offer investors a digitized form of a traditional ownership certificate, providing title of a regulated financial instrument combined with the agility and speed of blockchain. But there is so much more that security tokens can provide other than just proving ownership of title. The "digital wrapper" creates huge excitement because it will power a new era with widespread ramifications and possibilities for both investors and issuers globally. Not only will security tokens allow both old and new players to offer creative and original products and services but they will also bring about the cost savings and efficiencies made possible by digitization. Through process integration and superior design, security tokens will facilitate greater and wider access to new investor bases and new geographies that would otherwise be difficult to achieve.

The tokenization of securities is still in its early years of both development and adoption – mainly due to the complexities and uncertainties around regulatory compliance. Indeed, the transition to tokenization will not be easy. Security tokens are far more complicated than that of the cryptocurrencies on the market today. As a result, they will require more sophisticated applications for their creation, trading, and maintaining. Leading-edge technology companies are racing to build a new interconnected financial infrastructure on top of the blockchain to ensure tokens are safe, compliant, and more cost effective than the paper alternatives we deal in today. Regulatory bodies are watching closely and will move cautiously on what they allow – and the speed at which they move – so as to safeguard the public's interests.

The digitization of finance and security tokens is showing an incredible amount of promise. There are conceivably hundreds of trillions of dollars of assets worldwide whose value could be transformed and unlocked by the blockchain. The financial industry now has the products, the leadership, the systems, and the vision needed to make this potential a reality. Many stakeholders realize that there is something very big starting to unfold. Thought leaders and financial entrepreneurs are coming to accept that most assets can be digitized. Soon, the trading and ownership of digital assets will explode, and adoption will take hold. The ability to alter the liquidity, integrity, and cost effectiveness of a security will be the driving forces of this trend. The future and its potential are massive, and the growth will take place over many, many years.

The world is moving in a direction where blockchain will have a significant impact on how the markets interact. Players in the industry will need to have a broad comprehension of how the technology works, what it can affect, and what consequences it may have on business. The purpose of this book is to explain these concepts in a way for everyone to understand. Given that blockchain and security tokens have so much to offer, one of the biggest ironies is that education of the general public may very well be the greatest hurdle to going mainstream. Hopefully by the time you finish this book, you can safely say you have made it past that obstacle.

Disruption of Investment Industry

"The biggest opportunity set we can think of over the next decade."
Bob Grifeld, former CEO NASDAQ, discussing blockchain's potential[1]

So if blockchain and security tokens are so much better, cheaper, and faster than what we deal with today, does this mean "out with the old and in with the new?" Not exactly. This new way of doing things may not immediately replace lines of business currently seen in the financial space but will more likely provide powerful tools to help the overall industry grow and become more efficient. In short, the new technology will force change so that current systems must evolve.

Today, technology companies are rebuilding the financial infrastructure on top of here the blockchain, thereby creating a more efficient and interconnected financial fabric. This has led to the removal of many financial institutions from investment transactions in a way that is generally advantageous to investors and issuers. In the near future, there will likely be widespread attempts at disintermediation in which new companies and offerings will seek to disrupt the status quo by replacing the facilitators involved in many traditional business transactions with blockchain applications and services. These new ways of doing things are likely to usurp, disrupt and overtake the legacy competition.

Very much like the way the internet changed the financial services industry in the late 1990s, digital solutions will create new sales opportunities, new capabilities and new markets to tap. This innovative method of doing things will likely lead to cheaper, faster, and likely safer outcomes. Many of the services provided today will be very similar in their outcomes but will just be made better. Take the example of how the internet changed the way we buy an airplane ticket. Back in the day, if you wanted to travel from Washington, D.C to Berlin, you would contact your local travel agent and she would contact the appropriate airlines, search prices and get back to you with options. The tickets you bought would eventually be mailed to you. Today of course, you simply visit the website of an airline or go to an online travel booking site to do this. The internet merely made improvements – albeit significant improvements – to the old system. It created a faster and cheaper way of conducting business as usual. Likewise, as the internet opened up whole new realms of possibility, so too will blockchain.

Through the use of blockchain, security tokens are creating huge excitement because they can combine the best of the latest technologies with all of the investor protections and regulations that we find in traditional securities today. To cite just a few things that will be enhanced:

• Soon you may be able to move digital securities around the world 24 hours a day, seven days a week.

- Compliance systems will be embedded into securities and automated such that people can trade from jurisdiction to jurisdiction, without fear of running afoul of local regulators.
- Companies will be able to communicate with their investors all at once with just a click of a button. Corporate actions such as dividend payments, proxy voting, and rights offerings will be sent from the issuer directly to the investor.
- Investors will be able to trade in lucrative, often established, opportunities that lack liquidity today. For example, venture capital and private equity investments are often unavailable because of their lack of tradability and need for large ticket size. Security tokens offer avenues to alter that investor profile.

How Blockchain Will Disrupt the Financial Industry

While the removal of intermediaries and the automation of processes will generally be seen as advantageous to the economy and society as a whole, those who control the financial markets and their gateways will not go away quietly. Anyone who has been in business long enough knows the difficulty of disrupting the status quo. There are many entrenched constituencies who have strong incentives to resist change. Big businesses will scramble to keep things going their way. Regulators and legislators will look to ensure proper measures are in place to reduce risks and disruptions as the groundwork for blockchain is being implemented. As I discuss later in this book, it is essential to have guidance from both lawmakers and the large, most respected entities in the industry. Yet changes are coming and the technology isn't going away. As a result, initial resistance will be more of a speedbump than a barrier in seeing these possibilities unfold.

Case Study: Carlsberg

Based in Copenhagen, Denmark, Carlsberg A/S is the world's fourth largest brewer. In addition to its flagship namesake beer, the company brews world renown brand beverages Tuborg, Kronenbourg, Baltika, Grimbergen, Somersby Cider and more than 500 other beers. Carlsberg products are enjoyed all over the globe.

During my time as a portfolio manager of an international mutual fund based in the United States, I was an investor in Carlsberg on behalf of my clients. In order to build a position and hold Carlsberg stock, the following are just a few of the many steps that had to be taken:

Set-Up phase:
- A relationship had to be set up with a local Danish bank to act as a custodian for the shares
- A relationship had to be developed with a broker that had expertise in trading Danish securities
- A relationship had to be established with a broker specializing in foreign exchange with a particular niche to the Danish krone

Trading Stage:
- The fund's US dollars had to be converted into Danish krone
- Shares of Carlsberg had to be purchased on the Copenhagen stock exchange

Holding Stage:
- Carlsberg pays an annual dividend in Danish krone. Those dividends had to be converted back into US dollars before they were distributed to American clients.

A few other things to note. First, as I was based in Dallas and the stock was being traded in Copenhagen: the market hours were a factor of contention as trading of Carlsberg would be occurring late into the night for me. Second, American holidays and Danish holidays don't always coincide. If I were on holiday or the Danes were on holiday, there was little to no chance that we could've conducted trades during those times.

One could argue that we simply could have purchased Carlsberg in the United States as it has an ADR, or American Depository Receipt. Indeed, Carlsberg does have an Over-The-Counter ADR available. Unfortunately, issues arise in that scenario as well. At the time of this writing, Carlsberg stock in Copenhagen

(continued)

(continued)

saw over $30 million a day of stock traded on average; yet, the ADR traded less than $1 million some days. That is a significantly lower level of liquidity in the ADR and purchasing in the OTC market could result in a less favorable price than what could be obtained in Carlsberg's primary market of Copenhagen. Also, trading in the ADR market can be somewhat tricky especially around the dates when a dividend gets paid. Often times, the dates in which an ADR pays out a dividend is different from when the underlying stock does. Market makers in ADRs might be reluctant to exchange stock when there could be any question as to who gets the dividend. On top of that, the custodian banks who issue the ADRs can charge a handling fee that can be as high as 2% per annum.

This example illustrates how difficult and expensive cross-border trading and investing can be. While the fund I was investing for had billions of dollars under management and was able to bear cost, many smaller investors cannot. When making these investments, I often would scratch my head and ask "Isn't there a better way to do this?".

Legacy Ways of Doing Business

The financial systems used today are the summation of all things cobbled together in yesteryears. What does that mean? It means that when these systems were designed, the financial industry for which they were built looked different. The technology, service offerings and client demands were also different. It is not uncommon to hear of firms still using centralized mainframe computers or software systems from the 1970s for important processes. Thus, the designs of the systems used today are not running with what is available in today's markets for today's business climate.

Financial firms often have computer architectures that are multi-layered – there are different systems for the front, middle, and back offices. On top of that, you may have additional applications for handling financial, client or regulatory reporting. Manual inputs and manual corrections are standard in successfully completing many tasks. Financial entities will have entire departments dedicated to creating customized solutions to help these different systems talk to one another. As a result, information is not stored or handled in its most efficient way. These techniques lead to siloed workforces and unnecessary risk resulting in inefficient, costly, and sub-optimal business practices.

Paper Securities & The New Alternative

Paper certificates have long been the easiest and most economical method for recording and transferring ownership of securities. But this practice has led to issues including lost certificates, re-issued certificates, doubled up certificates and other problems. Numerous invalid or improperly handled security transfers have resulted in headaches for regulators, owners and issuers.

Digital forms of certificates will clarify the chain of custody and ownership. The financial industry will be shocked to realize how simple and superior the digital method is compared to what is used today.

In the late 1990s as the internet was first blossoming, regulators in the United States were in desperate need of a new way to collect and store the mandatory filings that were required of securities issuers. Instead of having to regularly process stacks and stacks of paper copies of filings, the regulators determined that electronic submission of all documentation was the better route. This led to the formation of the EDGAR database. Soon thereafter, all filings were required to be in digital form.

A similar type of reckoning may happen with security tokens. Regulators have much to gain by seeing an immutable, transparent record of the trade histories of securities and their holders. This digitization would lead to faster auditing, better monitoring and superior record keeping.

Historical Perspective: The London Whale

In 2012, a single trader lost almost $6.2 billion for JP Morgan. Nicknamed the "London Whale", the trader accumulated a position larger than what the bank would have ever allowed. When the market went against the trader, it was too late to correct the situation and losses mounted quickly.

Regulators investigated JPMorgan's internal controls and risk management systems. In the end, the bank was forced to pay nearly $1 billion in regulatory fines and a number of high-level executives took massive pay cuts.

A key reason that "The London Whale" was able to take such outsized positions was because some of the bank's risk measures were manually calculated on Excel spreadsheets.[2] While this practice is common in the industry, it is clearly inappropriate for such a mission-critical purpose.

A lot is riding on these financial systems. Undue risk is taken by not having integrated, reliable and trustworthy systems. Without proper communication protocols and processing capabilities, there is a significant risk that something important will fall through the cracks.

Financial institutions are led by some of society's smartest and most innovative professionals. These firms commit huge amounts of capital every year to ensuring they are competitive and up-to-date on compliance and regulatory standards. But revamping legacy IT systems can be a daunting task and problems associated with efficiency can get swept aside. There comes a time though when every business has to face the facts. The question of "Are we doing things right?" turns into "Are we doing the right things?". Financial institutions will have to come up with a new game plan and a new foundation on which to build their infrastructure. Blockchain, digital assets and security tokens can provide this definitive path for long run sustainability.

Entering the Disruptive Phase for Digital Assets

In the book "Bold: How to Go Big, Create Wealth and Impact the World", authors Peter Diamandis and Steven Kotler outline how advancements in information technology take hold in the marketplace. Diamandis and Kotler lay a framework for how these adoptions tend to unfold over the course of six very distinct stages they term "The Six Ds of Tech Disruptive Technology". The underlying thesis is that traditional industries will be shaken up as the world becomes more digitized, and that this will happen at an exponential rate. The authors' way of looking at how digital technologies become immersed into society help give us an idea of where digital securities are in their evolution.

> "The Six *D*s are a chain reaction of technological progression, a road map of rapid development that always leads to enormous upheaval and opportunity."
>
> Peter Diamandis and Steven Kotler[3]

As illustrated in **bold**, the six stages of exponential growth are as follows:

1. **Digitization** – Once boiled down into a series of ones and zeros, processes become an "information technology." This transformation enables new business models, products, services, or processes that can be supported by digital innovation. This turn of events marks a significant milestone for a line of business and sets about a chain reaction of incidents that challenge the traditional elements of that industry.
2. **Deception** – As things are digitized, time is needed before the innovation gets to a point where it can truly match its promised potential. During this stage, the growth is exponential but still seems relatively small to the public (think of the process of a penny doubling – after a few rounds, it has grown from 1 cent to 2 cents, to 4 cents, to 8 cents and so forth. More time is needed before an impact is really made). As a result, hype and interest around digitization can falter. Incumbent players in the industry will downplay the threat to their business. Society becomes impatient and begins to distrust what they once hoped for.
3. **Disruption** – Digitization increases the options for disruption. Entrepreneurs innovate new products and create new markets that will disrupt existing businesses. As more begin to realize the power the new way of doing things has to improve or optimize lives, the established customs and practices become obsolete – or at a minimum, less relevant. Unfortunately for those entrenched in the old ways of doing business, disruption always follows the deception period.

At this stage, either you disrupt or you will be disrupted by someone else – there is no avoiding the inevitable!

4. **Demonetization** – Here, money is removed from the equation and new offerings are free or offered at a fraction of their historical price. Costs of products and services fall dramatically. Two decades ago, a set of encyclopedias cost thousands of dollars; today Wikipedia is free, providing a more extensive, accurate, and update-to-date online alternative. Video editing software packages once sold for millions; now, people use Instagram apps.

5. **Dematerialization** – As digitization takes further hold, entire product lines disappear. Smart phone apps are the perfect examples – one phone can now replace the calculator, the camera, GPS, the alarm clock, the portable media player, and so many other devices.

6. **Democratization** – At this point, access to the new digitized product has become universal. On a recent trip to China, my mother and I were astonished to see Tibetan monks in the Dalai Lama's former residence in Lhasa using their smartphones to play prayer music! Even the remotes of the Himalayans did not stop the spread of handheld computers and the internet. This example shows how a technology's reach can eventually extend to anyone, anywhere in the world!

Dimandis and Kotler's roadmap is important to understand and plan for the disruptions likely to unfold in the financial industry. Blockchain is a foundational technology and is useful primarily for the apps that can be built on it. Security tokens are superior to what we use today because of their increased functionality and interoperability among many different financial applications and services. Developing this infrastructure is time intensive; but as the various components are being created, tested, and integrated with one another, the speed at which we will see the impacts on the finance business will increase. One of the inherent facets of information technologies is that their costs are often front loaded. They are expensive to construct at first but then they are extremely cheap to reproduce going forward. The groundwork for security tokens and blockchain has been laid over the last several years and is being perfected now.

"The Six *D*s of Tech-Disruptive Technology" posits that technology adoptions follow a predictable pattern. The framework seems to be playing out as scheduled with blockchain. Cryptocurrencies and utility tokens have shown the world the potential transformative aspects that digitization can bring about. A new era where digital replaces paper securities has come about slower than what people might have thought as some nefarious actors have used cryptocurrencies to further illicit activities. Hence, these signs show how we have been going through the deceptive phase of the "Tech-Disruptive Technology" sequence.

Now, blockchain and security tokens are entering the disruptive stage of their growth cycle. With the recent regulatory approval and exchange launching of several security tokens throughout the world, the digitization of securities will be followed closely by people at the forefront of the financial industry. Many of the digital products launched in past years, like cryptocurrencies and utility tokens, lacked the traits and integrations that are available today. The inclusion of these new features and improvements should provide opportunity for the public to reconsider the possibilities of digital securities. I believe that we are truly on the fringe of an era where this constantly evolving technology will amaze and overwhelm the financial industry.

Introduction Summary

- Blockchain technology will spearhead the next generation of financial market infrastructure.
- Blockchain provides a powerful way to transfer value and information between people without reliance on a third-party.
- Security tokens are a digitized form of traditional ownership certificates. They provide title of a regulated financial instrument with the speed and agility of blockchain.
- Blockchain and security tokens will disrupt the investment industry by providing cheaper and faster financial market solutions. These technologies will remove many of the middlemen from market transactions.
- Our current financial system is built on outdated and inefficient infrastructure. Blockchain technology provides a revolutionary means for bringing our markets into the 21st century.
- Blockchain and security tokens are entering the disruptive stage of their growth cycle.

PART I

THE MAGIC LEDGER

CHAPTER 1

BLOCKCHAIN BASICS

- Blockchain provides a highly effective means for exchanging value.
- Blockchain technology is made up of three main elements: accounting, computer science, and governance systems.
- Distributed ledger technology is the mechanism by which transactions are recorded and relayed to all participants on a blockchain.
- By design, blockchains are trustworthy, secure, transparent, efficient, and innovative.

What Is Blockchain?

Blockchain technology is a powerful means of exchanging value. A blockchain is a growing system – an interconnected list of records that are timestamped, secured, and agreed upon by such system's participants. The content of these records can include almost anything – amounts transferred, user information, details of terms behind each transaction, and really just about anything else pertinent to the transactions. A blockchain provides users the ability to access, observe, and analyze the data stored on the blockchain.

Foundational Elements of Blockchain

Blockchain stands on three basic elements: accounting, computer science, and governance systems.

Accounting

Ledgers In accounting terms, a **ledger** is used to keep track of money going in, out, and around an organization or system. The ledger serves as a diary to record the transactions and financial matters occurring over the lifespan of an organization or system. Blockchain is simply a digital ledger that records and logs the transactions of a community of users. Every participant maintains his or her own copy of this

FIGURE 1.1   A Simple Accounting Ledger

| Ledger Status A | | Ledger Status B | |
Name	Amount	Name	Amount
Francis	825	Francis	825
Sam	65	Sam	65
Rose	350	Rose	450
Scott	600	Scott	500
Paul	2,010	Paul	2,010
Total	**3,850**	**Total**	**3,850**

FIGURE 1.2   Sharing & Inspecting a Ledger

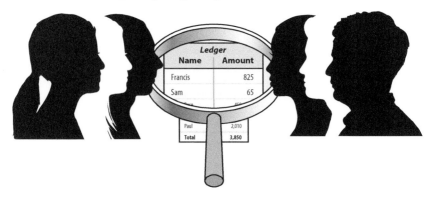

ledger. (See Figures 1.1 and 1.2) Updates of the ledger are automatically sent out to all participants. As an example, this simple ledger contains just two columns: names and amount.

Ledger A has 5 participants each holding a specific number of units. Suppose that Scott decides to send Rose 100 units. Scott will then have 100 fewer units and Rose will have 100 more units. Debit and credit entries are taken to reflect this change to the ledger and the total number of units in the system remains unchanged. By changing from Status A to Status B, the ledger is successfully updated and accurate. Despite the fact that just Scott and Rose were involved in this particular transaction, all participants receive and maintain a copy of this new ledger state.

Processing & Communications   Accounting not only measures what has occurred but also describes the processing and communication of financial and non-financial information across an entire entity. Take the case of how blockchain can be used to replace the role of a notary. Originally conceptualized in the early 1990s, blockchain was intended to be an electronic way to notarize documents.

Let's elaborate on this topic a bit more and understand how blockchain may be used to automate this process. As trusted third parties, notaries have played an important role in business over time as they act as official, unbiased observers and endorsers to a document's authenticity and validity. The duties of a notary may include the following:

- Identifying the parties involved and the provisioning of significant proofs of identities
- Acknowledging that the parties involved are of proper capacity to engage in what is intended
- Witnessing the state of a document
- Attesting to the seals and signatures contained in that document
- Recording the signatures along with the timing
- Delivering copies of the document to all relevant parties

Notarizing a document deters fraud and provides documented proof that a transaction is consummated under proper procedures, is complete in its entirety, and that parties involved are willing and aware at the time of execution. The notary process gives notice to all that the intended terms of a document are in full force and effect against the parties thereto.

Blockchain technology allows the duties of a notary to be written into computer code and performed by the blockchain itself, eliminating the need for a third-party notary.

The notary function is one of many accounting tasks that blockchain will perform. Blockchain can employ many other mechanisms from accounting to update and maintain the ledger referenced above. The digital nature of blockchain can facilitate the financial accounting, tax accounting, auditing, and reporting of activities that occur on the blockchain system. Through coding, just about any accounting procedure can be executed on the chain.

Computer Science

As mentioned earlier, computer science is one of the fundamental disciplines upon which blockchain technology is based. As a scientific field, **computer science** deals with how data is best handled, processed, stored, and communicated. As blockchain is based on the internet, a vast array of computer systems can be utilized to collaborate with one another on a global scale. As various subjects of computer science are employed and interact together, the resulting combination of technologies can create a synergistic effect and further enhance the capabilities of blockchain's potential. In this section, we will review selected topics that enable blockchain's attributes and abilities.

Networks **Networks** consist of two or more connected computers that work together for the purpose of sharing resources. The internet itself is a prime example of a network. Each participating computer in a network is known as a **node**. Individual nodes are assigned unique addresses to ensure all messages and connections are properly routed to the intended recipients.

Centralized vs Decentralized Networks are designed to be either centralized or decentralized. Centralized systems depend on one machine doing most of the heavy lifting. Advantages are that the system is relatively inexpensive, consistent, and requires little upfront time commitment. Changes or upgrades can be done quickly. In the early days of computing, most networks were centralized, meaning the majority of processing functions were carried out by a single machine in a remote centralized location.

Today most networks run off decentralized architecture. In a decentralized system, all computer nodes form the larger computer network. Many computers in use today have capabilities that far exceed the requirements of the business applications intended for them. Just to give this last statement some perspective, a modern smartphone is said to contain more computing power than what NASA had in its entirety in the 1960s when it put a man on the moon! As a result, many computers run relatively idle in comparison to their capacities and a decentralized system can utilize these spare resources to maximize efficiency.

Decentralized systems have numerous advantages. Decentralized systems can share files, peripherals, and other tools. Decentralized systems are more reliable than a centralized system since they are not prone to a single point of failure (i.e., they do not rely on one central node to complete a specific process). They are also scalable; if more resources are needed, you simply add more machines to the network.

Accessibility There are four known types of networks that blockchains run on today – public, private, hybrid, and consortium. The main difference comes in the form of "permissioning" – i.e., certain chains require consent to access particular features.

- Public blockchain networks have no restrictions whatsoever as to who can access them. If you can find an internet connection, you can participate in and validate the activities on the blockchain. Ethereum and Bitcoin are two well-known blockchain platforms that use public networks.
- Private blockchain networks require permission to join. Typically, a network administrator has rights to grant this access.
- Hybrid blockchain networks have a combination of characteristics from both public and private networks. Various factors determine the information on the blockchain that is made available to the public or held back for permissioned use. Dragonchain operates on a hybrid network.

• Consortium blockchain networks could be described as semi-decentralized. Access to the network can only be obtained with permission. However, control over the network is not governed by a single entity but instead by a group of approved parties. Corda, Hyperledger, and Quorum use this approach.

Databases   A **database** is a set or collection of structured information that is organized, stored, and accessed electronically from a computer system. Software applications known as database management systems (DBMS) are used to control and maintain most databases. This software serves as the interface between end users and the database itself, allowing the data to be easily organized, accessed, modified, updated, controlled, and managed. Like networks, databases can be centralized or decentralized and can be publicly or privately accessed.

Cryptography   **Cryptography** is the practice of securing communications via the processes of encryption and decryption to transmit messages between trusted parties. By using techniques from various disciplines of mathematics, physics, computer science, and other scientific fields, cryptography provides a method to ensure data confidentiality, data integrity, and authenticity.

One of the most commonly used cryptographic processes in blockchain is called hashing. With **hashing**, a message, regardless of its length, can be converted into text with a fixed number of characters. The messages in Figure 1.3 are encrypted with the SHA-256 hashing algorithm that is employed in all Bitcoin transactions.

The resulting values are called "hash values" or simply "hashes." Notice that all three results are the exact same length – 64 symbols. Also, if you study the cases more closely, you can see that Example A differs from Example B only in that the word "Blockchain" is made plural. By adding just one letter to example B, the subsequent hash is completely different – but still contains 64 symbols. Major changes to the result will occur if there is even the slightest change made to the string – adding one additional letter, changing one letter to uppercase, or adding a punctuation – it doesn't matter how subtle or great the variation is; the new result will change dramatically but still contain 64 characters.

FIGURE 1.3   Examples of Hashed Data

Example	Message	Hash Value
A	Blockchain	3eb95f8c5a596047754b4e5c13835f1d 27afcc4d80f10e83e17a047a6fdfbe30
B	Blockchains	9f74cef42d8240c88fb341b30a2cd08e 30ba126c171faa251adf2b06f13a6445
C	Security tokens are the wave of the future!	56092ab1327a86d0d4495fcfafb6a57d 7d34a9522c5e4dcea8723e2aa1ba79d5

Now let's look at Example C. This message is far longer, contains multiple words, and has punctuation. Regardless, the hashing algorithm reduces the results to the same number of characters – 64!

Hashing is used to convert a data set of an arbitrary size into one of a fixed size. The process employed is consistent regardless of who uses it; that same message always results in the same hash. Hashing can be executed quickly and ideally no two messages have the same hash value. These properties make hashing ideal for authenticating messages, detecting data corruption, discovering duplicated data, and identifying unique files.

Digital Identity The number of internet users worldwide now surpasses four billion and is increasing every year. Yet the tally of total devices is far greater. In 2018, the number of Internet of Things (IoT) devices surpassed the number of mobile devices.

The world wide web on its surface is fairly anonymous. With all of these gadgets and machines able to talk to one another, how can we be sure that we know exactly who we are communicating with? How can we be sure that the computer sending us messages or information is actually controlled by the person or organization it is claiming to be?

Some services on the internet require ways to determine the identity of a user. **Digital identity** is simply information that can be used to unambiguously identify someone or something online. Users may need or want to provide evidence of who they are and may be willing to provide documented evidence, such as a national passport or bank statement, to prove it.

Digital Identity of a User

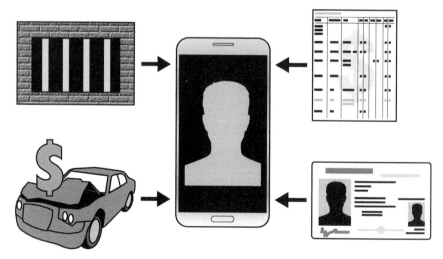

In the diagram above, the user has his background check, credit scores, driving record, and national ID card attached to his online profile.

A digital identity is often attached to one or more digital identifiers, like an email address, user ID, or domain name. As a user provides more sources of verified data to his or her profile, the credibility of the user builds and more direct access to services is allowed. Also, because the identity is in digital form, it can be easily transferred electronically to other businesses and for more purposes.

The development of digital identity creates multiple benefits for multiple parties. Users retain control of their accounts and can grow the number of identifiers as desired while maintaining say as to which parties they distribute their data. Businesses can reduce the risk of fraud, shorten onboarding times, lower client acquisition costs, and improve client experiences. Assets registered through a validated digital identity are protected by law and are thus in far better standing with regulators and government entities.

Digital Wallets   As blockchain-based options grow in popularity, most consumers will interact with these new applications through digital wallets. **Digital wallets** (sometimes referred to as "e-Wallets") are electronic devices or online services that allow users to make electronic payments, store digital securities, or maintain personal information. A wallet of this type can be linked to the user's bank account or other financial institutions (Apple Pay is an example). The adoption of these wallets represents a shift away from traditional methods toward electronic forms of transaction.

Digital wallets are gaining popularity worldwide as they provide enhanced user experiences in the form of increased convenience, security, and/or efficiency. Examples include:

Less to Carry: Depending on the type, digital wallets can offer features to store an abundance of information. This could include ID documents, health cards, membership cards, loyalty cards, and more. With digital wallets, life can quickly become "lighter" and more organized.

Less Wasted Time: Instead of fumbling around in the grocery store checkout line trying to find your debit card, loyalty card, and ID to verify your age, next time try making one tap or wave of your smartphone at the payment terminal to do all three! Checkout queues will become shorter as will the time it takes to getting on your way back home!

Fewer Forms: By having a digital wallet, consumers are not required to fill out paperwork each time they want to interact or transact with some other party. This is because their information has already been stored in the wallet and can automatically be updated and entered into the relevant forms needed to make a deal.

Enhanced Security: Wallet users also benefit because their information is encrypted or protected by a private software code; sellers can benefit by receiving protection against fraud. If a physical wallet is lost, whatever is inside is there for the taking!

So how does one remain confident that the contents of a digital wallet stay secure? A convention known as **key encryption** is one of the core elements of the blockchain's security structure. When a digital wallet is first created, two keys, one public and one private, are created. To put this into simple analogy form, think of this in the same way as when you might log into your favorite website or bank account. In this case, you will likely have a user name and a password. The public key is similar to the user name and can be shared with others. The private key is like your password and should never be given out. The public key serves as the wallet's address and gives the user a point of access to send and receive tokens to the wallet. The private key gives the owner access privileges to the wallet and its contents. Each time you make a transaction, your wallet's public key will be used to verify your identity and your private key will be safely embedded to process payments.

In the financial industry, wallets can allow users to leverage services for payment facilitation, compliance, identity management, token storage, and risk management. The features of wallets will create enhanced interoperability between all users of a blockchain community. Blockchain capabilities will allow for real-world identity checks to be made on the user that corresponds to a digital wallet in real time. Digital securities will have the ability to be held in a digital wallet as opposed to having to be housed at a traditional bank or brokerage firm.

Governance

The third critical element in understanding blockchain is **governance** – the sets of rules, processes, and relationships under which a system operates. These parameters shape the way participants use and behave under a system. Governance systems establish how decisions are made and identify the distribution of privileges and responsibilities of various participants. The following benefits occur under clearly established rules:

1. Long-term collaboration and strategic planning are encouraged.
2. Conflicts of interest between parties can be identified, mitigated, and/or avoided.
3. System maintenance costs are reduced.
4. Additional participants are attracted to the system.

Protocols **Protocols** are rules for electronic communication. In communication systems, such as blockchain, protocols are needed to move data across all types of networks, hardware, and software. Network protocols are programmed sets of rules that dictate the way in which information is treated and handled under a certain set of circumstances. They allow communications to be transmitted from one user to another.

Whether you realize it or not, you use protocols every time you use the internet. For example, they govern how emails are exchanged between one person who uses Hotmail and another who uses Gmail. In this case, Microsoft's Hotmail and Google's

Gmail may be products from different companies but through the proper use of protocols, they work together easily to deliver the end user the intended message.

To operate effectively, protocols have to be pre-defined and agreed upon in a communication network as standards. If protocols are not properly handled or rules are violated, communications will break down. Open and well-understood protocols become powerful tools to foster innovation and reduce costs.

Consensus   In order for a decentralized, distributed system to function properly, participants must reach agreement as to what transpires over the network. **Consensus** is the process by which participants come to a mutual understanding about what is published in the ledger. While this may seem trivial, it is vital to have rules governing how issues are sorted out in case of a dispute.

For example, in the game of soccer (or football as most people around the world call it!), it is forbidden for a player, other than the goalkeeper, to use his or her hands to touch the ball. That rule seems pretty cut and dry. In the 1986 World Cup, England and Argentina played one another in a legendary quarter-final matchup. In one of the most controversial plays in the sport's history, Argentina's Diego Maradona "headed" the ball over English goalkeeper Peter Shelton into the back of the net. This score ultimately gave Argentina what was needed to win them the game 2–1. Replay though showed the possibility, and likelihood, that Maradona used his hand to punch the ball over Shelton. To the English, Maradona was a cheater and the goal should not have been counted. To the Argentinians, the goal is sacred and Maradona is deeply revered as a hero. Forever remembered as the "Hand of God" play, Maradona's goal is still disputed to this day.

In the end, it was the referee's call and the goal went into the record books. Had fans and viewers been tasked to decide, we still might not have a champion from the 1986 World Cup. The ensuing gridlock between English and Argentine fans might never have ended.

Similar situations happen on a computer network just as easily. There can be disputes as to who is a legitimate participant, what transactions are valid, what transactions occurred, and what transactions did not. In a centralized system, one computer decides (as the referee did in the story mentioned above), but in a decentralized system, many opinions may have to be sorted out. When the stakes are high (and they usually are when money is involved), disputes are far more likely to happen. As a result, there have to be proper procedures and checks and balances in place to ensure all participants end up fairly treated.

Blockchains may differ from one another as to how consensus is reached; but nevertheless, adequate processes, protocols, and dispute remedies are vital to promoting a sustainable, trustworthy network. Currently, mechanisms like Proof-of-Work, Proof-of-Stake, Proof-of-Authority, Proof-of-Capacity and Adaptive Proof-of-Work (Tangle) are commonly used to establish consensus. Depending on which method is used, you might hear terms such as *mining, staking, forking,* or *validation* discussed as the process to achieve a consensus. While it is beyond the scope of this book to go into detail as to the exact way certain consensus mechanisms work, it is important to know that these methods are critical to maintaining and updating an accurate, agreed-upon ledger.

Distributed Ledger Technology

"We have elected to put our money and faith in a mathematical framework that is free of politics and human error."

Tyler Winklevoss, Co-creator of Facebook[1]

Many people ask the question, "Is there a difference between blockchain and distributed legal technology?" The terms are often used interchangeably but are not quite the same. Blockchain is just a type of distributed ledger technology. All blockchains are distributed ledgers, but not all distributed ledgers are blockchains and both give control of information and transactions to the users. Both are a type of database spread across multiple locations, nodes, or participants. The main difference is that distributed ledgers do not need to have transactions mathematically linked, whereas this added feature allows blockchain technology to offer a more secure and efficient way to create immutable logbooks (see Figure 1.4).

Still, distributed ledgers are incredibly useful in recording financial transactions due to the fact that they need no central authority. In today's financial world, most transactions must go through a clearing house. This forces society to "trust" these intermediaries and by extension, provide them compensation for their services.

FIGURE 1.4   Centralized vs. Distributed Ledgers

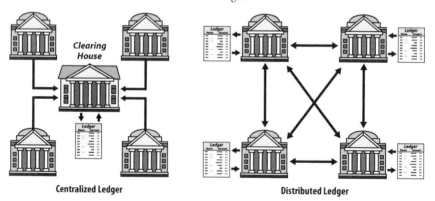

FIGURE 1.5   Data Fields Contained in a Block of Bitcoin

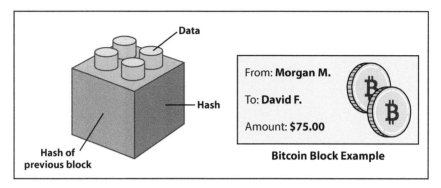

Distributed ledgers use consensus mechanisms among their users to replace this trust and eliminate the need for a single organization who oversees the data and its handling. This feature allows distributed ledgers to provide greater security, enhance efficiencies, and lower costs.

Building a Blockchain

Characteristics of a Block   So how is a blockchain formed as transactions take place? To begin, let's take a look at an individual block and what it consists of. Any single block will contain information that is mathematically encrypted through the process of hashing (as described earlier). Each block will contain three critical pieces of information: (a) the hash of the previous block, (b) data for the current block, and (c) a hash of the current block. The amount and type of data stored inside the current block is dependent on the fields relevant to the particular blockchain. Figure 1.5 is a visualization to help better create a picture of what is involved.

Linking a Blockchain Together   When a new blockchain is started, the first block must be unique. This is because there is no previous block to link it to. Called the "genesis block," this first block will be noteworthy as it does not contain a valid previous hash value. However, the data inside this block as well as this block's current hash value will be relevant to whatever unfolds in that transaction and will be formatted as normal. In the example below, notice with Block 1 that the "Previous Hash" is 000000 and the "Hash" is D98ATG. This block becomes the starting point on which all future blocks will be connected.

Once another transaction takes place, it will be time to produce Block 2. Encryption techniques will be employed to create new hash values for the new data

FIGURE 1.6   Example of a Linked Blockchain

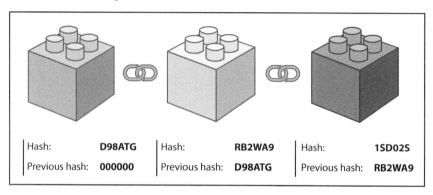

pertaining to that transaction. This new block will then be added to Block 1 and thus a "blockchain" is created. Notice how the "Previous Hash" of Block 2 is identical to the "Hash" of Block 1. Block 2 is thus forever connected to Block 1. The same will be true when Block 3 is produced; it will be forever connected to Block 2! This is one of the features that makes a blockchain so secure. This same process is repeated over and over again as additional blocks are connected to the chain (Figure 1.6).

This is a very basic technique of how blocks are created and chained to one another. There are more features that have to unfold to ensure a tamper-proof chain. Let's now build upon what we've covered so far.

Case Study: A Simple Card Transaction

Suppose you go out one night for dinner at a restaurant. At the end of the meal, you give your payment card to the waiter to settle up the bill. It would be easy to assume that it's just you and the restaurant involved in this transfer of money, but in reality, it is anything but. There are many interactions going on behind the scenes that ultimately add significant costs to your encounter.

Think about it – the card you hand over and the machine it is swiped or inserted through are both extensions of commercial intermediaries. To process your tab, your financial institution will run all relevant details through a series of channels. They will check your card's current balance and available lines of credit, anti-fraud detection measures will be employed, and other profoundly complex sets of issues will be resolved. Then, the restaurant's financial institution will run the transaction data through its own course of operations. If your financial institution differs from the one the restaurant uses, that will bring about a whole new set of problems to get worked out.

Depending on the circumstances, the list could go on and on. In the end, though, all of these go-betweens end up taking a big bite out of the restaurant's revenue and you, the consumer, will have borne some of that burden in the form of a higher sales price. Individuals, businesses, and society as a whole would greatly benefit if there were ways to eliminate these middlemen while still having secure, reliable, and trusted payment mechanisms. Fortunately, blockchain has many solutions to these problems already in place!

Creating a Blockchain Transaction

To understand better how value is transferred through a peer-to-peer blockchain network, we will now take a look at how a theoretical blockchain transaction could be executed from end to end. We'll reference the diagram below as we break down the blockchain processes into more easily understood parts. As we go along, try to notice how the blockchain itself and its automated processes eliminate the need for intermediaries (and their associated costs) while still providing a seamless, reliable, and trustworthy transfer of value.

Creating a Blockchain Transaction

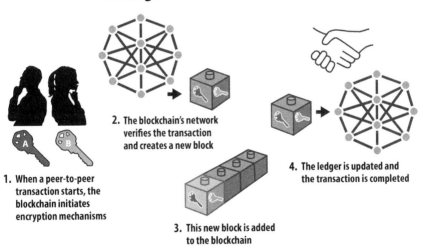

1. When a peer-to-peer transaction starts, the blockchain initiates encryption mechanisms

2. The blockchain's network verifies the transaction and creates a new block

3. This new block is added to the blockchain

4. The ledger is updated and the transaction is completed

Part 1 – A transaction begins when one party decides to send units of value to another in a peer-to-peer fashion. In this case, Alan wants to send 10 tokens to Beth. To make this happen, Alan will access his digital wallet and make a request to transfer the 10 tokens to Beth's wallet. Alan will need to enter Beth's public key address so that the tokens can be transferred to the right place. At this point, a series of processes will begin.

Alan's digital wallet will need to confirm that the person requesting this transfer is indeed Alan. Alan could enter his password or use biometric identification to provide verification. The wallet will check its balance to make sure Alan has a sufficient amount deposited.

The wallet will then take Alan's private key and feed it though a special crypto-graphic function that will create a **digital signature**. Like a pen-and-paper check, blockchain transactions require proof that the sender is indeed the real owner of what is being sent. Digital signatures are uniquely created in such a way that they can only be used in this one particular situation. They are encrypted so that others can-not forge them for fraudulent purposes in other transactions or at another time. The mathematical properties of a digital signature provide ironclad evidence to all users of the blockchain that it is indeed Alan who requested this transaction. Also, no one will be able use the digital signature to decipher Alan's private key.

Once these authentication procedures are finished, the wallet incorporates all of the request's relative information – Alan and Beth's public key addresses, a timestamp, the token amount, and Alan's digital signature – into the appropriate cryptographic hashes and formats. The resulting data will then be used to create a new block (Figure 1.7).

Part 2 – Alan's proposed block will now be sent to all participants on the blockchain. Every participant maintains his or her own copy of the blockchain ledger. Each participant will then check to see if Alan has at least 10 tokens in his account. The nodes will also inspect Alan's digital signature and look for any signs that the block has been tampered with. If everything checks out satisfactorily, each

FIGURE 1.7   Value Is Transferred from Alan to Beth Through the Blockchain

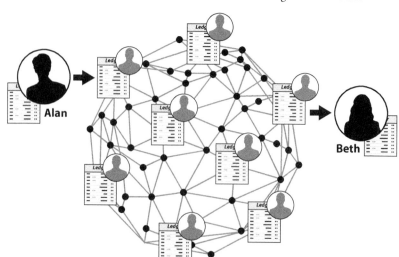

participant should approve the block, its contents, and thus the transaction itself. The blockchain will look to all participants to determine whether consensus has been reached. If so, this means that everyone is in agreement with the new state of the ledger and the block is ready to be connected to the existing blockchain.

Part 3 – The newly confirmed block will be connected to the end of the last version of the blockchain. The added block is now cryptographically linked to existing blocks.

Part 4 – The new updated blockchain is complete and everyone will get a copy of the latest version. Because the process is conducted in a digital manner, all participants will simultaneously be sent the freshly made ledger.

Tampering with a Blockchain

So what happens if someone tries to fraudulently alter the contents of the ledger? Let's look at some reasons why this is nearly impossible to achieve on a widely used blockchain.

Before getting into specific scenarios, let's step back and examine the big picture. One of the primary reasons people gravitate to blockchain solutions is because one avoids interference from central authorities as everyone holds a copy of the ledger being used. The data and its history are mathematically encrypted and distributed through a peer-to-peer network over the web. The participants themselves can reject blocks that have delinquencies or hashes that are inconsistent with what their version shows, creating a self-policing mechanism.

When someone tries to alter the ledger, a message is broadcast out to inform everyone of the intention. If someone purposely attempts to manipulate the contents of the ledger even slightly, the hashes of the blocks would no longer line up. Remember that making even a minor change in the data will cause a major change to the resulting hash. Nodes on the blockchain could spot these differences quickly and reject the proposed changes. And without a consensus, the ledger may not be altered.

Let's examine a few cases as to how and why someone could try and tamper with a ledger:

A participant could want to forge copies of tokens to make new ones to spend.
  After all, digital assets are just a series of zeros and ones. But that isn't enough to make new tokens out of thin air. On a blockchain, ownership and the scarcity of an asset are concrete and clear. If someone attempted to place additional tokens in a particular account, the ledger where this change is made would then be out of sync with all the other ledgers on the system. Other users of the chain will reject that version and refuse to grant the request. So in order to change the number of tokens in any particular account (up or down), valid transactions will have to take place – and each transaction requires mutual agreement from the network to be included in the ledger.

A participant may try to spend more tokens than are in his or her account.   Whenever a request to transfer a certain number of tokens is made, the entire community of users checks the ledger to confirm whether a sender has enough tokens in an account to cover what is being sent. If the account is insufficient, the transaction is stopped right away and nothing will change in the ledger. The intended receiver will not see an increase in the account balance. The checking mechanism prevents what is known as the **double-spending problem**.

A participant may try to send multiple transactions simultaneously and may not have have enough to cover the sum amount of all the requests. In this case, suppose Kim has 100 tokens in his account. At the same time, he sends 75 tokens to Lee and 50 tokens to Pat. But Kim only has 100 tokens and is thus short 25 tokens. Blockchain transactions are always ordered before they are processed. So, one of these transactions or the other will be put in the queue first despite the fact Kim sent both out at the same time. Blockchain platforms may vary as to how positions are determined, but there will be always be a sorting mechanism that will rank the order in which requests are processed. In this situation:

- If Kim's transfer to Lee goes first, Lee will get the 75 tokens and Kim will be left with 25. The transaction to Pat will end up getting rejected due to insufficient funds in Kim's account. Pat will get nothing.
- If Kim's transfer to Pat goes first, Pat will get the 50 tokens and Kim will be left with 50. The transaction to Lee will end up getting rejected due to insufficient funds in Kim's account. Lee will get nothing.

   Remember that whoever is left out under these circumstances will quickly learn so. The lack of an increasing value to either Lee's or Pat's account will tip them off that Kim has not fulfilled his end of the bargain. Kim will then have to reconcile with the excluded party. The community on this blockchain avoids the issue of double-spending.

A participant could try to invalidate a prior transaction. In this case, the members of the community could look at the previous blocks and determine that it did indeed happen. Mathematically structured data would show the specifics of the completed transaction and is found via evidence such as timestamps, digital signatures, and consensus agreement by the network. Just as if the prior owner of a house came back and re-staked claim, the real owner could produce notarized documents and reference official government record archives to show verification that the sale happened and was in full force post a stated date.

A participant may try to intercept the tokens. A member may try to take these tokens for his own, but the other participants would not accept a fraudulent taking. By altering the address where the tokens are going, this changes the contents of the message in the block. The resulting hash would be different from what was intended and would not be able to pass the necessary validation checks needed for approval by the community.

Nodes on the block try to charge a fee or tax on an account whose owner did not authorize the withdrawal. Remember, tokens leaving an account need to be authorized by their rightful owner. In this case, the extracted tokens would not contain the proper digital signatures. The true owner of the account would need to authorize the digital wallet containing the tokens to send out additional funds in order for fees and taxes to get collected.

A participant sends a bogus transaction to only select members of the network community for verification while other participants are left out. In this case, the ledgers that received the fake transaction would be out of sync with those that did get wind of what happened. The inconsistencies in ledger status *could* prevent a consensus from occurring.

The mathematics and distributive nature of blockchain are what make the technology solid. When it comes down to it, just about the only way to falsify what is contained on a blockchain would be to get an overwhelmingly large portion of the network's participants to form a consensus around a false ledger. But as more and more people have the same copy of the ledger, it would become increasingly difficult to pull off such a conspiracy.

In the last example above, the inconsistencies would prevent a new consensus from occurring but there is the possibility that if enough nodes are convinced to agree on the false state of the ledger, the group may become large enough to have an overwhelming ability to force consensus. So while a broken system is not totally out of the question, factors such as the robustness of the programming behind the blockchain platform, the reputation of the community on that platform, and the precise procedures employed in the consensus mechanism are so important to keeping the system functioning as intended. While it may be possible to compromise one or even a few individuals, as the number of members in the community increase, it becomes harder and harder to pull off a scam. That is one of the great beauties of blockchain – as the community grows, so too does the strength of its integrity.

Smart Contracts

Contracts are an essential part of any properly functioning business. Contracts legally define ownership rights and create obligations between the various parties involved. These agreements provide the parties with a validation of understanding, terms of exchange, and remedies in the event of disputes. Unfortunately, when a party to a contract does not follow the terms of the agreement, the other party might try to negotiate with the breaching counterparty or might seek resolution in court. Anyone who has experienced these types of legal proceedings knows just how costly, time consuming, and unsettling they can be.

One of the most useful and powerful capabilities of blockchain is the ability to use smart contracts. **Smart contracts** allow for logic to be programmed on top of transactions; in essence, they are units of computer code that execute a set of commands when certain predefined conditions are true. At a basic level, smart contracts perform calculations, store information, or send transactions based on the terms of a contract. Through a series of "if/then" statements, smart contracts become self-executing and self-governing. This protocol facilitates the verification, implementation, and enforcement of the underlying contract all without the use of any intermediaries.

How Smart Contracts Work

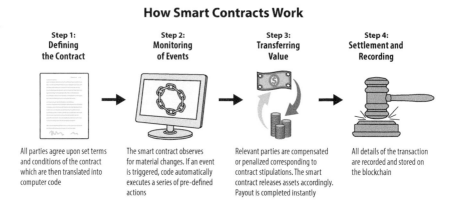

Step 1: Defining the Contract	Step 2: Monitoring of Events	Step 3: Transferring Value	Step 4: Settlement and Recording
All parties agree upon set terms and conditions of the contract which are then translated into computer code	The smart contract observes for material changes. If an event is triggered, code automatically executes a series of pre-defined actions	Relevant parties are compensated or penalized corresponding to contract stipulations. The smart contract releases assets accordingly. Payout is completed instantly	All details of the transaction are recorded and stored on the blockchain

Oracles

In order to foster increased autonomy and reliability, smart contracts can be executed depending on data received from an outside source. An **oracle** is an agreed-upon and trusted third-party data source. Through the use of oracles, smart contracts determine if, how, and when its contractual terms have been adequately fulfilled. As a result, oracles open up immense possibilities to use realy-world data and information as a condition for the automatic execution of a contract.

> **Case Study: AXA's Flight Delay Insurance – "fizzy"**
>
> European financial behemoth AXA has developed a product called "fizzy" that uses the Ethereum blockchain to create an insurance contract for customers inconvenienced in the event of a flight delay. The concept is rather simple: fizzy is completely automated; interested clients can visit AXA's website and get a quote after entering flight details. Then if the policyholder's plane is delayed two or more hours, whatever the cause, fizzy will immediately provide compensation based on the terms of the policy.
>
> The fizzy platform is connected to various air traffic databases around the world which act as oracles and the smart contract accesses all relevant information to determine if indeed a delay has occurred. With the use of smart contracts, fizzy decides the outcome of the policy based on a simple set of "if/then"-type rules. If the oracle posts the flight's landing time as greater than two hours after the scheduled arrival time, payment to the policyholder is triggered. As a result,

both the policyholder and AXA have delegated the reimbursemen͟ an independent set of agreed-upon third parties.

The coverage provided is totally transparent in that everyone knows in advance exactly how much will be reimbursed if a flight is delayed. The blockchain technology provides ironclad trust that the contract's terms cannot be changed after the policy is purchased and that the insured will get paid if conditions are met.

With most standard insurance products, the onus to prove an event and its damages is on the policyholder. But in the case of fizzy, the policyholder isn't required to prove anything. The smart contract makes things highly convenient – customers are alleviated from the stress of having to provide documents detailing the delay. Verification and payments are done automatically by the smart contract and the programmed code behind it. This saves an incredible amount of time, effort, energy, and haggling – for both AXA and its clients. It also cuts down, and practically eliminates, the potential for fraud.

Fizzy is a great example of how transparent and easy doing business can be with the use of smart contracts. It's no wonder AXA hypes fizzy with the slogan "No need to ask for it, no paperwork, no wasted time."[2,3]

Smart contracts have incredible utility for users to structure and execute transactions ranging from the simple to the highly complex. Smart contracts can be used to exchange money, property, rights, securities, or anything of else of value in an open, hassle-free way. When the smart contract has been fulfilled, payments deposited in escrow accounts are released. Smart contracts define the rules and penalties around an agreement in the same way as a traditional contract, but automatically enforce the obligations without any other actions needed by the parties involved. Once executed, the results of a smart contract are encrypted onto the blockchain and then stored for recordkeeping in an immutable way.

In the end, smart contracts enable autonomy and the creation of instant trust between parties. Investors love – and reward – certainty and transparency. When people commit capital for long periods of time, they want to know what they're getting. Smart contracts define exactly what to expect and ensure that exactly what is defined actually transpires. Users may rest assured that terms will be fulfilled and validated on a timely, accurate, and auditable basis. Smart contracts also create the opportunity for large savings for participants – the money spent on intermediaries is now retained by the parties.

Smart contracts need no discussion, debate, or waiting. The computer program will run just as it was coded to do, on time, every time. Given the ease and certainty of this way of doing business, many believe smart contracts will become the backbone of the global transaction system. (See Figure 1.8.)

FIGURE 1.8   Benefits of Smart Contracts

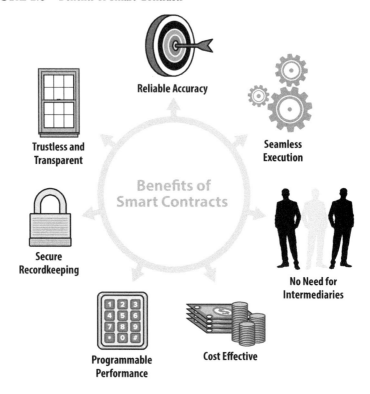

The Characteristics and Benefits of Blockchain

> "Anything that can be conceived of as a supply chain, blockchain can vastly improve its efficiency; it doesn't matter if it's people, numbers, data, money."
>
> Ginni Rometty, CEO, IBM[4]

Now that we've taken a good look at the ways blockchain works and what it can do, it's time to summarize the key takeaways as to why this is the technology for the future of the financial industry.

Benefits of blockchain:

Trustworthy

- A network of users provides self-policing over the activities on the blockchain.
- Coded procedures enable a uniform method to track and verify all data stored on a chain.
- Users have a proven outlet to control their own data, assets, and identity.

Secure

- Key encryption protects the rights of the individual users; at the same time, cryptographic functions ensure that everyone can view the contents of the ledger and its history.
- Mathematical rules ensure that the records kept on the chain are tamper-proof and permanent.
- The decentralized nature of the network prevents any single points of failure from comprising the data or operations of a blockchain. This makes blockchain less susceptible to fraud and cybercrime issues.

Transparent

- As the platform is not centrally controlled, the system should remain neutral and unbiased.
- Network of participants openly conduct transactions on a shared ledger.
- When any participant wants to transmit a message, the block is sent to all the peers. No particular entity can stop that from occurring. Thus, censorship should not be problematic.

Efficient

- The benefits of blockchain operating in a digital domain create a multitude of opportunities to streamline processes, eliminate manual interventions, and automate tasks like auditing, reporting, and notarizing.
- Cost reductions and quicker processing times can be realized as middlemen are cut out.
- Predefined rules can eliminate or mitigate disputes between participants.
- Technology can reduce risk and increase accuracy rates.

Innovative

- The architecture of blockchain allows engineers to build upon it. This ability enhances the interoperability of new and existing applications and facilitates coordination between all the moving parts. Smart contracts are an example of the potential these interconnections can bring.
- Blockchain is adaptable, as upgrades and other enhancements can be undertaken when needed.

While there are many words and phrases that might be used to describe blockchain, one that might stand out as an overarching characteristic is "integrity." The technology provides a reliable, consistent, safe, and customer friendly way of performing many types of transactions, More and more people, businesses, and organizations are implementing blockchain solutions to drive cost reductions and to open opportunities for new business models and revenue streams. These economic incentives will cause an explosion in the number of eager adopters looking to harness blockchain for years to come. The financial industry is already seeing that happen!

What Differentiates One Blockchain Platform from Another?

The blockchain revolution began in 2009 when the world was first introduced to Bitcoin. Since then, multiple attempts have been made to add more features, redesign, and improve its capabilities. Completely new blockchains, sometimes referred to as **blockchain platforms**, have been set in motion – some have broader use cases, some have different technical applications, some might have more restricted access, some have a combination of those and other facets. When it comes to selecting which blockchain solutions will win out in terms of gaining market share, there are several factors to consider. No platform is perfect. Just like when a consumer looks to choose a new car, many tradeoffs have to be weighed. There is no one-size-fits-all option in blockchain – at least not at this time.

Today, Bitcoin is the predominant choice on the market. It has a strong user base, but its technology is lacking when compared to other blockchain systems. Ethereum has a niche with its smart contract features but many have questioned whether it has the transaction throughput capacity to be sustainable in the long run. EOS has better scalability than either Bitcoin or Ethereum but hasn't been able to win over adopters. There are many other choices and more will debut in years to come. Let's take a look now at some topics and questions that need to be asked in determining if a blockchain has the features to make it appealing for mass adoption.

Purpose

- What is the blockchain intended to do?
- Is this purpose unique in the marketplace?
- Are the purposes of the blockchain too wide or too narrow?

Community

- How widely used is the platform? Will the usefulness of the platform increase as more people adopt it?
- How diverse is the user base?
- What kind of reputation does the platform have?
- Is this platform conducive to tech professionals investing time in its development?
- Are proper protocols established that could encourage developers and new users to come to this platform?

Capabilities

- How do the various features of the platform add value to users?
- How reliable is the platform?
- What are the critical limitations of this platform?
- Does the underlying technology support smart contracts and decentralized applications?
- Is the platform sustainable for long-term usage?
- Are the applications and features on the platform compatible with other widely used technologies?
- Can the platform easily be modified or upgraded to include new technologies or features?

Usability

- Is the platform user-friendly and easy for new participants to engage with?
- Does the network require permission before users can access it?
- Are there any concerns that regulations could affect the way the platform is used?

Integrity

- How secure is the blockchain itself?
- Are there issues around privacy?
- Does the consensus mechanism provide proper incentives and promote fairness?
- Are the procedures conducted on the platform sound so that transactions cannot be forged or altered?
- How is relevant data stored and accessed?
- Is the supply of tokens for the platform fixed or can the number be changed based on the interests of certain parties?

Economics

- How much time is needed for transactions to be added to the chain? Will this speed be affected as the user base changes in size?
- Are tokens for the platform available to trade on important exchanges?
- Are there fees associated with transactions? What other costs might be incurred while using the platform?
- Is it energy intensive to publish new transactions to the ledger?
- How easy is it to convert the underlying tokens into fiat or other digital securities (and vice versa)?

When evaluating the various blockchain platforms, aggregate benefits, costs, and risks should be considered. It will be important to contemplate everything not only from your own perspective but also through the eyes of others. Think about this through the framework of how you might predict the potential winner of a talent competition. To do so, you have to think about the characteristics that someone else or the group in its entirety would gravitate toward.

Chapter Summary

- Blockchain provides a highly effective means for exchanging value.
- The three elements that provide the foundation of blockchain technology are accounting, computer science, and governance systems.
- Cryptography serves as the basis on which blockchain messages are disseminated.
- Distributed ledger technology is the mechanism by which transactions are recorded and relayed to all participants on a blockchain.
- Smart contracts can facilitate the automatic exchange of value without the need of an intermediary when certain conditions are met. This functionality can be embedded into a blockchain.
- By design, blockchains are trustworthy, secure, transparent, efficient, and innovative.
- There are currently thousands of blockchain platforms available on the marketplace today. The most widely known are Bitcoin, Ethereum, Ripple, and EOS. Blockchain platforms can have different features, capabilities, and use cases.

CHAPTER 2

FUNDAMENTALS OF A SECURITY TOKEN

- Security tokens will provide greater functionality, lower costs, faster speeds, and increased transparency to financial markets.
- Digital securities are categorized as either payment tokens, utility tokens, or security/asset tokens.
- Tokenization is the process whereby the rights to a real-world asset are converted into a digital security that can be housed, subdivided, and traded on a blockchain system.

Distinguishing the Types of Digital Assets

It's been more than a decade since the first blockchain-enabled digital asset, Bitcoin, was launched. Since then, the world has realized the widespread ramifications and possibilities this new technology brings in the form of creating new investment opportunities, raising capital for projects, and even reducing regulatory risk. But as new "cryptos," "cryptocurrencies," "alt-coins," and other tokens were designed to solve many specific real-world problems, significant differences in the purposes and characteristics of these tokens have become apparent. The use and functionality of tokens can vary widely and as a result, basic classifications needed to be made to distinguish the way these products are used and regulated.

A clear framework has been established to help differentiate among these offerings. Thought leaders and regulatory bodies have generally concluded that three classifications of tokens are appropriate when dealing with digital assets. In 2018, the Swiss regulator FINMA took action to develop a concrete set of criteria to define the guidelines and parameters in making the distinctions.[1] Following FINMA's lead, other parties have generally come to accept these standards in the marketplace. As a result, a general worldwide consensus has evolved and digital securities (more commonly known as "cryptocurrencies") have been divided into the categories of **payment tokens**, **utility tokens**, and **asset tokens**.

Let's take a look at each of these categories in more detail and in doing so, view each through the lens of their specific characteristics, the different rights they convey, the ways in which they are regulated at a high level, and the mechanisms necessary for their transfer. While all three types of tokens are made possible by blockchain technology, each type is fundamentally different.

Payment Tokens: These tokens are simply a form of digital currency and act as a medium of exchange and as a store of value. Mathematical properties and governance mechanisms are used to generate new units and verify the transfer of units. This category was designed to be the simplest of the three types of tokens.

Payment token values are determined solely by supply and demand. The price action will simply be a function of how much buyers want it versus how much sellers don't! Obviously, the price of the token increases if the number of users of the token increases, and vice versa. On the supply side, if more tokens are issued, the price will go down, and vice versa.

Bitcoin and other cryptocurrencies were created based on the idea that a market free from interference should exist and that anonymity of the users should be respected. Payment tokens were coded such that they would operate independently from a central authority. Therefore, it has been extremely difficult to enact meaningful regulations to inhibit their transfer.

> "If the United States were to decide – and I'm not saying that it should – we don't want cryptocurrency to happen in the United States and tried to ban it, I'm pretty confident we couldn't succeed in doing that because this is a global innovation."
>
> United States Senator Mike Crapo, Chairman Senate Banking Committee[2]

Utility Tokens: These digital assets enable their holders to interact with or gain utility from a platform. Utility tokens are not created as investments; the tokens do not provide any ownership rights in the underlying project nor do they give any ability to control how decisions around the underlying entity are made. They merely enable the holder to interact with the services the entity has stated it will provide.

Utility tokens could be used to access network data storage, to process certain data through a specialized algorithm, or to play an online video game. The uses and possibilities are many.

The simplest way of thinking about this classification might be to compare these tokens to those you might use in an amusement park. When I was growing up, we would go to the State Fair and fork over cash at the admission gate to obtain several golden coins – each would entitle us to a ride on one of the Fair's attractions. When we wanted to go on, say, the ferris wheel, we just handed over one coin and the operator would let us in. Though the coins were clearly marked "No Cash Value," they did have worth in that they provided us with rights to do what we desired.

Utility tokens behave much the same way as what we bought at the State Fair. In no way did buying a coin give us the right to tell the State Fair's management what rides to have, what prices they could charge, or whom they must hire. Nor did these coins give us a part of the profits that might have existed at the end of the day. They were simply a way to derive use of a specific service.

Utility tokens can and have been used to fund the creation of a project. This is where investors have to be careful. Often, utility tokens have been created as a type of pre-paid voucher for a service to be provided following the creation of a certain project or infrastructure. Too many times, promoters have sold the tokens but never gone to the trouble of developing what they advertised. This would be like buying tickets or tokens for the State Fair and it never coming to town or delivering the types of rides promised. Caveat Emptor!

The values of utility tokens are driven by simple supply and demand and rely on the faith of their users to maintain worth. Generally, transferability is controlled in the same way as payment tokens. This can vary case by case and often Know-Your-Customer and Anti–Money Laundering rules might apply.

Generally speaking, the level of regulation that falls on utility tokens is fairly minimal and lies somewhere between what is required of payment tokens and security tokens. Depending on the jurisdiction, some levels of protection may be required but probably not much.

Asset Tokens: These are also widely known as **security tokens**. These tokens are linked to and constitute an economic claim to a real-world asset. Security token holders are entitled to certain rights and privileges of the underlying property. This could include distributions of earnings, proceeds from the asset's sale, dividends, or spin-offs. Holders may be eligible to vote on the managing of the asset or have the ability to demand an accounting of any events that have transpired. Almost anything of value – be it real estate, commodities, art, intellectual properties, fixed income instruments, or just about anything else – can be used as collateral for a security token.

One of the key understandings of a security token is that its price interacts with the value of the assets underlying it. Suppose a security token is linked to one ounce of gold. If the price of gold on an exchange is $1,000 per ounce, then the theoretical price of the token should be $1,000. If the price of gold goes up by $50, then so should the value of the token.

We will address regulation in-depth later but to summarize, regulation is quite strict for a security token. High standards apply at many stages, including in the token's creation and transfer. These tokens can only be released after meeting stringent legal and compliance hurdles; this provides the public with investor protections mandated by government authorities. If applicable laws are not followed, the issuers and investors may be subject to criminal proceedings and/or other penalties.

You may also hear a token called an "**Alt-Coin**." The term is simply short for "alternative coin" and means that the token is an alternative to Bitcoin. Because of it's dominant market position and popularity as the first cryptocurrency offered, *Bitcoin* is often used as a generic term for all tokens. Alt-coins are simply platforms that offer tokens on a blockchain like Bitcoin does. Other than their distinction from

FIGURE 2.1   Token Categories & Characteristics

Token Type	Payment	Utility	Security
Examples	Bitcoin, Ethereum	Binance, Chainlink	BitBond, Aspen St.Regis
Characteristics	Provide Medium of Exchange and Store of Value. Avoids security-like features	Avoids security-like features	Exhibit security-like features
Rights	Claim to Tokens Only	Use of Service Rights	Establish Ownership Rights
Regulation	Difficult to Regulate by Design	Limited Regulation	Extensive Regulation
Transferability	Virtually No Restrictions	Limited Restrictions	Subject to Wide Array of Restrictions including AML & KYC Requirements, Clauses Embedded into Smart Contracts and Other Rules

Bitcoin, the term *Alt-coin* really doesn't imply much else. Alt-coins could theoretically be payment, utility, or security tokens. Primarily, though, alt-coins in the marketplace today are payment tokens. (See Figure 2.1.)

How Security Tokens Came Along

Today when most people think of digital securities, they immediately associate that term with the word "crypto." Up to this point in time, the investment and trading of digital assets has mostly focused on these currencies functioning as payment tokens. But the foundational technologies of blockchain are spreading to other types of assets at a rapid rate. Soon, the market for security tokens will dwarf that of payment and utility tokens combined. How did we get to this exciting moment in the history of finance and what events had to unfold to make this happen?

It took several years after its creation for Bitcoin to really build a following and it wasn't until 2012 that its transactions exceeded more than 1 million per month.[3] Over the following years, more cryptocurrencies were issued but the news in the space was largely dominated by scandals and government crackdowns on nefarious dealings. Regulators and law enforcement in places like the United States, China, and South Korea began to figure out how to deal with this new phenomenon that seemed to be sweeping the globe. Since the release of Bitcoin, over 4,000 alt-coins have been released.[4]

Overstock.com was one of the first well known e-commerce sites to accept payment for its goods through the transfer of Bitcoin. The company conducted extensive due diligence before making the decision to accept cryptocurrency and in the process of doing so, they determined that another potentially beneficial use of blockchain technology would be the tokenizing of debt and equity securities. As a result, CEO Patrick Byrne invested heavily in the research of security token trading.[5]

Innovative entrepreneurs joined in and explored how security tokens could shake up the way markets worked and looked for profitable ways to monetize and develop its potential. Soon, tokens began to be issued with Know-Your-Customer and Anti-Money-Laundering features to bring them more into compliance with best practices. Later, tokens were enhanced with digital identity technologies that lifted their legitimacy.

Other major milestones came when regulatory bodies announced the rules around the various classifications of digital securities. In 2014, the UK Treasury was commissioned to study cryptocurrencies and determine what role they might play in the British economy as well as to evaluate whether legal guidelines needed to be applied.[6] In June 2018, the US Securities and Exchange Commission (SEC) ruled that neither of the cryptocurrencies Ethereum or Bitcoin would be classified as a security. The rationale for this was that these platforms were highly decentralized. However, other types of utility tokens and payment tokens would fall under the control of the SEC and thus would be subject to relevant securities laws. This decision was significant; had the SEC ruled otherwise, innovation in the space would have been stifled.[7]

In July 2019, the SEC cleared blockchain start-up Blockstack to issue the first regulated security token under crowdfunding rules.[8] In September 2019, the Seychelles-based MERJ Exchange became the world's first blockchain firm to initiate an IPO on a national stock exchange.[9] These events are evidence that tokenization can work with the necessary regulatory mechanisms for the safe and compliant issuance of a security.

We are starting to see a wave of new companies and projects funded through security tokens. Pioneering entrepreneurs are deciding to list their offerings with this innovative wrapper format. Eventually the tokenization of traditional securities will begin to take place and offer an incredible host of benefits that will change the way the financial market infrastructure operates.

As security tokenization becomes more widespread and the digital wrappers around them become more standardized, the overall cost of administering the security over its lifecycle will drop. Security tokens will open new capabilities and will eliminate many of the hassles associated in dealing with investments. This creates a massive opportunity for ventures conducting the issuing, buying, and selling of these digital securities.

Tokenizing a Security

The tokenization of traditional securities will provide a multitude of benefits that will revolutionize how financial markets work. **Tokenization** is the process whereby the rights to a real-world asset are converted into a digital security that can be housed, subdivided, and traded on a blockchain system. By going through this process, the ownership of the asset is digitally linked and tracked through the token. This procedure does not change the nature of the asset itself but rather enhances the way its ownership is tracked and managed.

Security tokens are the digital product that is created when an asset is tokenized. Security tokens use decentralized control to oversee the recordkeeping, transferring, and authenticity of the underlying assets. The decentralized control over each security token works through distributed ledger technology and, in particular, blockchain that will serve as a transaction database. By allowing tokens to administer the storage and management of an asset, it becomes easier to track, record, verify, and trade the underlying property.

Historical Perspective: Gold Certificates

Benjamin Franklin said that there are only two certainties in life: death and taxes. One of the most consistent forms of tax that governments impose on their citizens comes in the form of inflation. This levy on wealth is as old as the hills. In ancient times, the Roman government decided to hollow out the center part of the silver coins in circulation to help prevent a shortage of precious metals. Of course, the senators also mandated that the value of the coins would remain the same despite their lower metal content!

People can't be fooled with these types of tricks for very long and will start to make adjustments to their behavior rather quickly. When there is too much money chasing too few goods, prices start to go up. If governments don't stop legislating money out of thin air, prices can spiral out of control and the currency that serves as legal tender is no longer accepted by anyone. In the last one hundred years, nations all over the world from Germany, to Hungary, to Venezuela, to Zimbabwe, have all seen their economies (and the life savings of their people) wrecked by inflation.

During the Civil War, the United States government was spending enormous amounts of money to fund the war effort. As is typical when governments overspend, inflation kicked in and people began to lose faith in their fiat currencies. This is exactly what happened to the US dollar.

As a result, the US Congress took measures to restore a viable means of exchange in the economy. But given Uncle Sam's track record during that era, real changes had to be brought about to restore confidence in the money supply. In 1863, the first gold certificate in the United States was issued in the form of paper currency. Each certificate gave its holder the right to redeem a corresponding amount of gold. For every $20.67 of currency that was issued, one troy ounce of gold would sit in a vault to ensure the bearers of these gold certificates could render their paper money in exchange for bullion.

This system worked for many years and restored trust and faith to the economy. People could rest assured that the paper certificates they received in exchange for the goods and services they rendered would provide a store of value.

Unfortunately, the politicians in Washington couldn't quite keep their budgets in line and at various times, they devalued the dollars (and thus the gold certificates) relative to gold. In 1933, President Roosevelt issued an Executive Order which suspended the gold standard except for foreign exchange and revoked gold as a universal tender for debts. With his decree, gold was then worth $35 per troy ounce and this value stood for almost four decades. Then in 1971, in the face of a huge foreign trade deficit, President Richard Nixon shocked the world and unilaterally ordered the cancellation of the dollar's convertibility into gold. People took notice and very quickly inflation soared again. The price of gold rose to over $650 per troy ounce by 1980.[10]

There are many reasons why the gold certificate system failed. But in the end, the real reason for the loss was rooted in the fact there was no way to ensure trust and to remedy the situation when the government did not fulfill its end of the bargain.

Today, the American dollar is solely backed by the "full faith and credit of the US government" and this ideal is the basis of virtually every other currency issued throughout the world. That doesn't quite have the same ring as "it's Good as Gold"!

A digital token backed by an asset really is not that much different from what the government did with its gold certificate program. So what went wrong with what the government did and why should security tokens fare any differently? Throughout this book, consider how smart contracts, distributed ledger technology, and segregation of duties around issuance, custody, and reporting would assist in preventing tokenized assets from the same fate as the gold certificates.

Code Is Law

It is likely no coincidence that Bitcoin and other blockchains were developed and caught the public's attention after the Global Financial Crisis of 2008. Those perilous times exposed many systematic flaws in our financial system and showed just how sensitive and fragile our most trusted institutions were. As a result, society began to distrust our market structure, its central bankers, and the politicians who legislated regulations. To some, the individuals who oversaw our financial exchanges were seen as bad actors; a group not to be trusted. This environment led some to look for ways to overhaul the system. This undoubtedly led to the beginnings of Bitcoin and blockchain financial products.

One of the most alluring features of digital assets is that distributed ledger technology can help us to address the issues of transparency and liquidity. By programming rules into the securities themselves, greater oversight, access and transparency are derived. The computer code behind these rules can be relied upon to prevent malicious intentions, manipulations and unnecessary speculations in the marketplace. Predefined rules can help us to better embrace compliance, data protection and automated real-time reporting. Coding and open information prevent any central figure from suddenly diluting the worth of something or slowly fleecing its value over time. Essentially, blockchain provides a way to return monetary and economic power to the people.

Benefits of Tokenization

We will now take a look at some of the enormous benefits security tokens possess.

Benefits of Tokenization

| Process Automation | Continuous Trading | Faster Execution | Asset Interoperability |

| Fractional Ownership | Increased Liquidity and Market Depth | Flexibility of Smart Contracts | Cost Efficiencies |

Process Automation – Security token technology will allow a number of service functions that are currently carried out by paid third-party intermediaries to be automated through use of the blockchain. Many of the steps to exchange and maintain a security have historically been low-value additives as well as expensive but necessary from a regulatory standpoint. The technology of blockchain will allow these processes to be executed seamlessly by code embedded into the security token itself. Costs will be reduced as a result and the savings will be shared by a plethora of stakeholders.

Through security tokens, ownership and the transfer history of the underlying security will be digitally recorded on the blockchain. By digitizing and standardizing title of possession, administrative efforts around recordkeeping and transaction reconciliation will be streamlined. In today's market where paper certificates are the norm, it can be difficult to move in and out of an asset since ownership documents are often disjointed. It may be that some official papers that provide proof of ownership are locked in a safety deposit box or kept in a file cabinet. Others might be stored as PDFs electronically. It is also not uncommon that these documents get lost and therefore need to be replaced. On top of it all, business and legal documents require numerous signatures or the actions of a notary to be legally valid. With tokens, all that is necessary to validate ownership and the steps for appropriate transfer are programmed into and contained within the security itself. When an owner wants to sell, the transaction is quick, cost-effective and hassle free.

Smart contracts allow the holder to directly interact with the token's underlying business or asset. Corporate actions such as voting or buyback rights will be executed routinely and the token holders' responses could be shared. It will be possible to automate dividends and distribute them at more frequent intervals than just annually or quarterly.

In summary, automated processes will reduce costs, enhance capabilities, and create more accountability.

Continuous Trading – Believe it or not, there are frustrations around the limited trading times under which the various exchanges operate. If you want to trade a US stock in today's marketplace, you typically can do it on weekdays between 9:30 a.m. and 4:00 p.m. Eastern Time. That's assuming the day you want to trade isn't a market holiday. Also, this assumes you live in the eastern time zone; if you live in California, you have to wake up early to put in a trade at the open and markets are closed by the time you're done eating lunch. Then there are people who live in places like Hawaii or Alaska or even another country – let's just say those folks face even more inconveniences in trading US securities!

Theoretically, you can trade security tokens any time of day, any day of the week. As security tokens trade in decentralized markets (as opposed to being listed on national exchanges), transactions will not be constrained to the standard operating hours of an exchange. Buying or selling will be conducted whenever and wherever!

Faster Deal Execution – When making a deal, speed can be critical. Typically, a transaction will take longer to consummate as more and more people are involved. As security tokens remove intermediaries from transactions and automate necessary processes, the time it takes for an issuer to successfully offer a security will be accelerated. On top of this, the time it takes to execute a trade and subsequently make settlement can be reduced to just seconds.

Asset Interoperability – As digital technologies can be engineered to work with one another, the possibilities of various assets and processes interacting with one another are tremendous. Let's take the example of a home mortgage. When a homeowner buys a house with credit, the title to that property will be encumbered with a lien. Once the owner has paid the loan in full, the title will have to be cleared and properly recorded in the appropriate government jurisdiction. With today's standard ways of doing business, this can take a lot of time to complete and includes a boatload of manual work. With a security token, it would be possible to automatically release the lien once the loan balance is paid off and then electronically execute the documentation needed to create a clear title. This could dramatically reduce some of the closing costs that occur when a house is sold.

In this last example, one asset, the mortgage loan, is interacting with another, the title to the house. This concept of interoperability could be applied to other important types of financing options. It could be used whenever there is collateral for lending, pledging, or in other creative monetary techniques.

Fractional Ownership – The ability to fractionalize assets through tokenization will bring a flood of liquidity into markets where average investors have historically had little or no access. If you can afford to buy a luxury property or a high-rise building all to yourself, congratulations! But let's say you wanted to invest in that same property except in this case, you would only own a portion of it. That is extremely challenging to do in today's environment. It would require incredible amounts of paperwork and legal advice. You could buy exposure to a basket of these types of properties through a REIT (real estate investment trust) or traded holding company, but these likely wouldn't give you the specific property you may want.

Fractionalization opens markets to smaller investors, allows segmentation, and removes the need to transfer the underlying title of many assets. The splitting up of ownership leads to lower minimum investments and again will help increase liquidity.

Increased Liquidity & Market Depth – The opportunity to monetize assets will be expanded dramatically because of tokenization. Today many securities are illiquid because of regulatory concerns or because the cost of transfer is simply too high. The process for tracking trade activity can be manual, costly, and place a significant strain on issuers who need to protect themselves from regulatory risk. Legal fees mount quickly when the appropriate paperwork has to be drawn up. Because of this lack of flexibility, many private securities are often sold at a discount and thus fail to capture the full value of the underlying asset. However, projects that structure their owner-ship with security tokens may allow investors the option to find liquidity at a more suitable time.

Chapter Summary

- The use and functionality of tokens varies widely and as a result, basic classifications needed to be made to distinguish the way these products are used and regulated. Digital securities have been categorized as either payment tokens, utility tokens, or security/asset tokens.
- Tokenization is the process where the rights to a real-world asset are converted into a digital security that can be housed, subdivided, and traded on a blockchain system. By going through this process, the ownership of the asset is digitally linked and tracked through the token.
- Security tokens can use decentralized control to oversee the recordkeeping, trans-ferring, and authenticity of assets.
- Security tokens and distributed ledger technology help to address the issues of trans-parency and liquidity. By programming rules into the security tokens themselves, greater oversight, access, and transparency are derived.
- Security tokens will provide greater functionality, lower costs, speedier transactions, and increased transparency to financial markets.

WHAT TYPES OF ASSETS MAY BE TOKENIZED?

- Tokens can be created to represent ownership in fiat currencies, bonds, equities, funds, as well as a slew of additional asset classes.
- Asset-backed tokens constitute the economic rights to real-world assets like commodities, art, real estate, or infrastructure projects.

The digitization of the financial industry will have a profound impact on how we trade securities, how we maintain shares throughout their lifecycle, and will even provide additional choices in which we can invest our money. By using security tokens rather than the traditional paper stock certificates to represent securities, our financial system will be far more efficient and offer tremendous new advantages. This innovative process opens up the possibility of unlocking trillions of dollars of investable assets to new investors, provides the potential to increase the volume of trades of such assets, and reduces the friction involved in the creation, buying, and selling of securities.

Tokenization is already taking place in many areas of the market. In this section, we'll see what types of assets are already available in digitized form, what assets are likely to be tokenized, and then analyze some key facets of this exciting new breakthrough.

The Move Toward Tokens Backed by Assets

While the growth in value of Bitcoin, and some other cryptocurrencies, has been nothing short of spectacular, Bitcoin's price has seen dramatic swings which have been too much for most investors to stomach. Declines in excess of 50% or more have been fairly common. The fluctuations in Bitcoin's worth relative to the US dollar is based on many factors; ultimately, though, Bitcoin is a speculative asset and its demand is the primary driver of its value. This volatility has created many challenges for people who need to place an equivalent fiat value on their crypto holdings. These gyrations also prevent goods and services from being exchanged in cryptocurrency. Why would an item be priced at one Bitcoin if the seller knew the value of what she was receiving could be $8,000 today and possibly $6,000 tomorrow? This makes Bitcoin and other cryptocurrencies too risky to currently be used as a medium of exchange.

Stablecoins

Stablecoins are cryptocurrencies designed to have reduced volatility as their price is often linked to a stated "stable" asset or basket of assets. In most cases, stablecoins are pegged either to fiat money or a commodity. With these attributes, stablecoins have payment utility and do not serve as just a speculative store of value. Stablecoins with redemption features for their underlying asset are said to be "backed"; on the other hand, those that are not redeemable are referred to as "seigniorage-style." In today's markets, most stablecoins have a controlling body that manages and monitors the tangible assets that serve as the peg underlying the issued tokens.

So how might a typical stablecoin work? Let's illustrate with an example of a digitized dollar, one very similar to some of the leading options offered on the market today. *Keep in mind, though, each stablecoin will offer different terms of service and procedures. This illustration is of a theoretical stablecoin.*

Let's suppose in this hypothetical case that every token in circulation is collateralized 1:1 with the U.S. dollar. The token's controlling body verifies that reserves are held in deposit by a variety of approved and affiliated financial institutions (often called "on-ramps" and "off-ramps"). These reserves are then independently audited and reported on a frequent, say monthly, basis to ensure the public that the tokens are indeed backed on a 1:1 basis with deposited cash.

Stablecoins are created and redeemed dynamically; for every dollar deposited with an affiliate bank, another new unit of token is issued. To place money into the system, an investor will deposit funds with an on-ramp financial institution that has been approved by the token's controlling body. That on-ramp will then execute a series of protocols to turn the cash into a digital equivalent that is pegged to the value of the deposit funds. The customers receive the subsequent token and are then free to transact with the stablecoins to facilitate digital purchases as they wish, just the same as they would with US dollars. Newly minted tokens adhere to the same properties of existing tokens. The on-ramp will hold the deposited amount in dollars until such amount is redeemed at a later date.

Redemptions go through the above protocol in reverse. Tokens are "burned" or destroyed when a customer delivers his tokens to an off-ramp. Upon successful verification and validation, funds from the underlying cash reserves will be transferred to the customer's external bank subject to the token's terms and conditions of use. Each

FIGURE 3.1   Hypothetical Stablecoin Flow of Funds

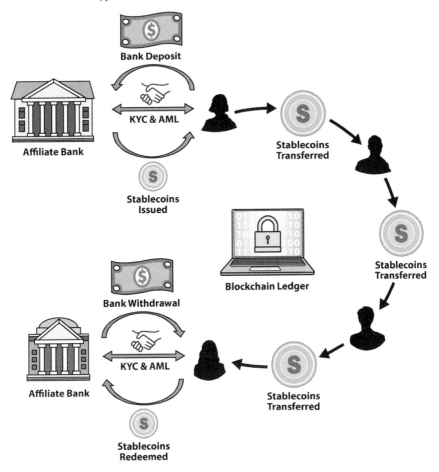

step of the process is designed to keep the balance between the tokens in circulation and the total value of the deposited currency equal (Figure 3.1).

As a result of the token's design, the market value of one token should then be equivalent to the amount of fiat assets in reserves backing it – in this case $1; and it should stay at or very near to this amount over time. Imagine what would happen in the following situations:

- If the token's value on the open market deviated below $1 to say 95 cents, someone would buy the token on an exchange and quickly redeem them at an off-ramp so to receive $1. This would result in a profit of 5 cents for every token run through this process. This situation would not last for long because market participants would exploit this profitable opportunity until it is no longer available. The number of tokens in circulation would decrease and the demand for the token on the open market would increase. This buying and redeeming would stop once the open market price hits $1.

- On the other hand, suppose the token traded on the market at $1.05. Investors would deposit $1 in an on-ramp to create new tokens. These new tokens could then be sold on the exchange for $1.05. The investor would make a profit of 5 cents for each token run through this process. This situation would not last for long because market participants would exploit this profitable opportunity until it is no longer available. The number of tokens in circulation would increase and the demand for the token on the open market would decrease. This issuing and selling would stop once the open market price hits $1.

In both of these cases, the supply and demand for the token changes very quickly such that the market price will gravitate back to $1. In the world of finance, this practice is known as *arbitrage*.

Stablecoins could allow users to move money anywhere in the world in minutes instead of days in a cheap and secure fashion. Tokens are an important foundation for the development of payment facilitation, lending solutions, risk management, and the trading of digital securities. As stablecoins representing fiat currencies become more popular, users will be able to hold digital forms of euro, British pound, Hong Kong dollar, Japanese yen, and theoretically any other currency. This will allow for huge amounts of real money to be imported into the system and subsequently transferred around the digital ecosystem anytime, anywhere.

In today's market, some of the most popular stablecoins representing US dollars are Tether, USDCoin, Paxos Standard, TrueUSD, and the Gemini Dollar.

Case Study: Facebook's Libra

One of the most talked about stories of 2019 in blockchain was Facebook's decision to launch a digital payment token called "Libra." The idea seemed simple enough: based on the same principles as a stablecoin, Libra's value would be backed by hard assets. Its value would be maintained by placing the funds users paid to acquire the Libras into bank deposits and other cash equivalents. Facebook signed up an all-star list of brand-name corporate titans from around the globe – each of whom paid $10 million to partner in this new project. Libra seemed like it would be an unstoppable force that would jumpstart digital adoption to the mainstream (Figure 3.2).

FIGURE 3.2   Libra Association Network of Partners

Source: Libra Association[1]
*This image is accurate as of April 1, 2020

Facebook touted that Libra would have numerous benefits: it would help to provide financial services to the unbanked, it would cut down on the fees individuals and small businesses paid to process transactions, and it would make the problems associated with cross-border payments a thing of the past.[2] With billions of Facebook users worldwide and established communication channels, Libra seemed incredibly well positioned to succeed where other cryptocurrencies had failed.

But Facebook's announcement was not met with open arms. Regulators from Europe, China, the US, and other countries immediately raised objections ranging from concerns over money laundering, to customer protections, and the credibility (and even ability) of a tech company like Facebook to manage this massive financial-based undertaking. Some read between the lines and thought the governments' intentions were even broader: Could it be that central bankers and politicians were worried that Libra would eat away at the dominance of the US dollar and other fiat currencies?

(continued)

(continued)

My initial inclination was to think that Facebook was doing something that others had already done. It was copycatting what Tether, USDCoin, and other stablecoins in the marketplace had been doing for well over a year. Having done more research, I realized that that was not the case. Facebook was not pegging the value of Libra against one currency, say the US dollar, but rather against a basket of many financial instruments they could be denominated in many different currencies. This creates all sorts of problems for Facebook, its users, and possibly for society as a whole.

Why? One of the main requirements of a currency in general is that it possess three critical features: a means of exchange, a store of value, and a unit of accounting. Libra unquestionably meets the first two. But as for the third, Libra is not a unit of accounting. Remember what Benjamin Franklin said about death and taxes? Regardless of who you are or how you do business, you do ultimately reside in one country and doing business there means that government is going to tax you. The problem with Libra is that its value will fluctuate as the values of the underlying assets backing it – the currencies, the bonds, and other marketable securities – fluctuate.

Take the following example:

1. Brenda buys 100 Libra for $106.
2. Brenda then goes and spends those same 100 Libra four days later at her favorite restaurant in Seattle. However, the value of Libra has since changed in the marketplace such that 100 Libra are now worth $108.

In this example, a tax agent could easily determine that Brenda made a profit of $2 on her "investment" in Libra. Come Tax Day, the tax agent will have his hand out to collect his portion of that profit. You can quickly see how this creates problems for anyone using Libra. Would the same not happen if you bought shares of Amazon, for say $100,000 in 2009, and then used them as payment in exchange for a $2,000,000 home ten years later? Libra potentially creates an accounting, reporting, and tax nightmare for anyone who touches it.

Also, by maintaining a pool of various assets that would be used to meet redemption requests from Libra, Facebook would effectively be running a money market fund. Those funds require SEC registration and extensive AML and KYC compliance (more on this later). Most troubling is what might happen during a market panic similar to what occurred in 2008 when many money market funds could not meet redemption requests. Perhaps the same could happen with Facebook during a crisis. Should something like this unfold, the US federal government and probably the governments of other nations would have to step in and provide a guarantee to the money market funds. This would mean the taxpayer, or the broader society as a whole, is on the hook. As a result, Facebook might have to be treated as a bank and regulated as such. There does seem to be some validity to the politicians' concerns and issues will have to be worked out before Libra can move forward as Facebook initially envisioned.

The real silver lining to this story is that when Libra signed up heavyweights in the payments space like MasterCard, Visa, and others, it gave significant credibility to blockchain use in digital payments. It forced a major discussion about digital currency and payment processing in the press, among individuals, and even in the highest halls of power in major countries. If, how, and when Facebook releases Libra is still up in the air.[3] The ideas and theories behind Libra are fundamentally sound; however, changes in the mechanics of how the currency operates, will have to be made before it can pass regulatory scrutiny and thrive. Regardless, stablecoins as a whole are growing in assets and usage, a trend that will most likely continue.

Other big-name sponsors are considering moving into blockchain-based payments. Walmart, the largest retailer in the US, has applied for a blockchain-based digital currency patent. From what the headlines are saying, it looks like Walmart has embraced the ideas behind a digital currency and realizes the enormous savings that could occur (and that it and its customers would benefit from) with the use of digital currencies. Walmart's offering could also be used as payment at select retailers or partners. In this case, the US dollar would be the only base currency and would eliminate many of the confusions and hassles that Libra presented.[4]

These examples provide clear evidence that the broader market is moving toward greater acceptance of digital assets. This is a necessary step for society as a whole to embrace this technology in greater numbers.

Asset-Backed Tokens

Asset-backed tokens constitute the economic rights to real-world assets like commodities, art, real estate, or infrastructure projects. The assets themselves that are underlying the token are held in the form of a trust, by a custodian, or by the entity promoting the token. The token contract may or may not offer a redemption feature permitting the holder to take physical delivery of the underlying asset.

Commodity tokens provide digital proof of ownership of commodity assets like basic or precious metals, agricultural commodities, or petroleum products. As with stable coins, each token issued is backed by a fixed ratio of the corresponding commodity that is held in deposit by the custodial bank. These may be a good option for someone looking for direct investment in commodities or as a safe store of capital. These instruments are popular because they provide an easy way to gain exposure to something like silver or oil without having to deal with the cumbersome issues around the transportation, storage, or insurance of the physical commodity. The investors will usually bear a fee proportional to the total costs incurred by all participants in the vehicle. Typically, independent auditors will carry out checks as to the quantity, quality, and location of the underlying commodities. The issuance and redemption of the commodity tokens likely follow procedures similar to those of the digital monies described above.

Case Study: Britain's Royal Mint

Founded over 1,100 years ago, the Royal Mint of Great Britain produces coins and medals for the United Kingdom and 60 other countries. The Royal Mint also secures precious metal bullion in its highly secured facility known as "The Vault."

It may be ironic that this 1,000+ year old institution would be interested in cutting-edge technology; but the Royal Mint has created a new innovative product using distributed ledger technology to allow investors direct ownership of physical gold bullion. The gold is held in the form of fully allocated, segregated London Bullion Market Association, or LBMA, gold bars within its secure storage facilities. The Mint now offers ownership of this gold through tokens on the blockchain. The Mint calls this tokenized security "RMG" and each token represents ownership of one gram of real gold.

What makes the RMG token interesting is it there are no ongoing management fees or storage costs associated with holding the gold, and the tokens are issued by a well-known, time-tested stalwart in the gold space. These tokens provide a secure, flexible, and cost-effective way to invest and trade in gold. The distributed ledger will allow the Royal Mint to know exactly who owns the gold it has in its custody. Token holders have the benefits of real-time pricing and 24/7 access to trading on secondary markets.[5]

Case Study: St. Regis Aspen Resort

In the world of commercial real estate, we are starting to see where tokenization is being used to finance projects. The St. Regis Aspen Resort is a mountain ski lodge located in Colorado. The resort has roughly 180 guest rooms and has over 20 private residences associated with the property. The hotel is an internationally renowned ski destination known for luxury and high-quality service.

The company that controlled and managed the St. Regis Aspen Resort found a new way to raise money for this project by issuing security tokens that were compliant with SEC regulation. The company decided to have digital share certificates as opposed to the old-fashioned less versatile paper ones. The tokens provide a way for investors to own a stake in an iconic Colorado property.

Tokens were sold for one dollar each through an offering called Aspen Digital. The property itself, the St. Regis Aspen Resort, was sold into an operating partnership and the tokens issued represented ownership in that partnership. Over $18 million worth of tokens were sold to institutional and accredited investors representing ~19% of the equity portion of the deal. The minimum purchase size was 10,000 tokens. The deal was structured by a firm called Elevated Returns.

The developers of the project were looking to create an investment structure where the hotel could be sold as a single asset Real Estate Investment Trust. The initial public offering, or IPO, was lauded as the first of its kind in the United States. As an offering of just $20 million was not scalable through the traditional route of an IPO, the promoters decided to use tokenization to take the asset public. They saw the direction in which blockchain and digital securities were going and realized the benefits in this innovative path. This deal will certainly be looked upon as a blueprint for how future real estate deals can be financed through security tokens.

"It's a beautiful instrument because all of the security's regulations are actually embedded into the contract itself. It's cheaper and faster to transact and offers also the ability to have a global product trading on multiple exchanges worldwide." Comments about Aspen Digital by Stephane De Baets, President, Elevated Returns[6]

Fixed Income, Equity, and Funds Tokens

Bond-Like Tokens – These tokens are backed by debt instruments and constitute a claim on its income streams and principal payments. As the terms of a fixed income instrument are typically less complicated than in those for equities or derivatives, bond-like tokens are relatively easier to automate through the use of smart contracts. Their structure can be set up to eliminate the need of intermediaries and registries. Tokenization can help to reduce settlement times and operational risk.

Case Study: IBM's Blockchain Accelerator

Corporate giant IBM is looking to build the world's first debt issuance platform that uses blockchain technology. The market for corporate debt is in excess of $80 trillion and often includes private issuances of fixed income securities. With the current infrastructure, these instruments can be difficult to track, price, and trade. With the aid of new distributed ledger technologies, IBM is hoping to provide modern methods to streamline and simplify this important form of financing![7]

Case Study: The World Bank's Bond-i

In August 2019, the World Bank issued 50 million Australian dollars of bonds with a one-year maturity. This global organization worked with the Commonwealth Bank of Australia and Canadian banks RBC and Toronto Dominion to create this new offering. The Bond-i is part of a strategic focus of the World Bank to foster disruptive technologies that prove beneficial to its clients. The World Bank saw blockchain as a creative way to streamline its processes for raising capital and trading securities; they believe that distributed ledger technology will also help it to improve its regulatory oversight.

This fundraising event marks the first time that the World Bank has utilized this new blockchain platform. Going forward the bank plans to issue more bonds in this fashion. The distributed ledger technology will be used for the creation, allocation, transfer, and lifecycle management of all new bonds, thus creating an intuitive solution to improve operational efficiencies.

> "Commonwealth Bank of Australia now has tangible evidence from our first bond offering using blockchain technology and subsequent bond management, secondary trading and tap issue via the same platform, that blockchain technology can deliver a new level of efficiency, transparency and risk management capability versus the existing market infrastructure. Next, we intend to deliver additional functionality to deliver greater efficiencies in settlement, custody and regulatory compliance."
>
> Sophie Gilder, Head of Blockchain & AI, Commonwealth Bank of Australia[8]

Share-Like Tokens – In this case, security tokens are issued to act like stocks on the blockchain. These tokens provide ownership-like features that grant stakes in entities like a corporation or limited partnership. Depending on the particular deal, share-like tokens can offer dividends, profit shares, or other interests in the entity. Tokens can enable their holders to voting rights and other privileges.

Revenue share tokens would likely fall into this category. Revenue sharing agreements are contractual incentives that provide various parties to a specifically defined portion of an entity's revenue stream. For example, a revenue sharing agreement could provide a landlord with 6% of the gross revenue of a restaurant that operates out of property she leases. Businesses that rely on revenue percentages for royalties, mineral rights, real estate contracts or key employee compensation agreements have turned to security tokens to create a more seamless solution to deal with cash flows. The utilization of smart contracts make security tokens ideal for this type of sharing arrangement. However, revenue sharing agreements typically do not classify as either debt or equity but still do provide a claim on a percentage of the gross revenues for an entity.

Chapter 3 What Types of Assets May Be Tokenized?

Industry Trends: Alternative Financing with Security Tokens

One of the most interesting trends in blockchain comes in the form of alternative financing. Tokenization offers the potential to create more complex products and avenues to innovate. As tokens have enhanced flexibility and transparency when compared to traditional forms of ownership, they are ideal for creativity and opening up new, exciting investment products.

DREAM Fan Shares

The world of sports is no stranger to the digital space. Did you know that as early as 2014, the NBA's Sacramento Kings began taking Bitcoins as payment for tickets and merchandise? The Kings are not the only athletic club taking part; here are a few other teams and athletes looking to hop on the blockchain wave:

- European football clubs like Juventus, Paris Saint Germain, West Ham, and Roma are utilizing blockchain to help fans engage with their favorite players.
- Barcelona superstar Lionel Messi has served as a spokesperson for various crypto and blockchain endeavors.
- The Miami Dolphins have designated Litecoin as their official team cryptocurrency.

These digital interactions with fans will likely cause additional adoption of blockchain![9]

Here is another new and interesting idea – want to help your favorite professional athletes kickstart their off-court entrepreneurial career? DREAM Fan Shares has developed a platform to support the issuance of tokenized securities to capitalize on the income streams of athletes, artists, and influencers.[10] In October 2019, NBA player Spencer Dinwiddie announced his intentions to create a debt offering worth up to $13.5 million and make them into tradable digital assets. The guard for the Brooklyn Nets signed a three-year, $34 million contract and sought out investors who would pay him cash upfront based on his ability to repay these notes. Investors receive monthly coupons that result in a yield of roughly 5% interest per annum. This arrangement marked the first ever Professional Athlete Investment Token (PAInT).

The PAInTs are hosted on the Ethereum blockchain and Paxos Depository Trust administers all cash flows in their PAX stablecoin. Investments are only available to "qualified investors," subject to a one-year lockup, and represent a general obligation on Dinwiddie's creditworthiness. Investors are expected to receive bond-like payments from Dinwiddie as he collects his earnings from the NBA and other endeavors.[11] The issuance of security tokens backed by the economic wherewithal of a professional athlete offers a glimpse of how tokenization may be used as an innovative way to monetize revenue streams.

FAT Brands Franchise Revenue Bonds

California-based FAT Brands is the parent company of restaurant chains Fat Burger, Bonanza Steakhouse, and Ponderosa Steakhouse. In March 2020, the company issued almost $40 million worth of tokens through two bond offerings on the Ethereum blockchain. The company trades on the NASDAQ stock market; as a result, the firm could have likely tapped the traditional credit markets for funding but instead saw tokenization as a better way obtain capital. The company plans to use the revenues it receives from its 380 worldwide franchisees to back the value of the newly issued bonds. FAT Brands believes that by tokenizing its debts, investors will have a better mechanism to receive clarity around the company. Also, the issuance is expected to save the firm almost $2 million in annual interest expenses.

> "The digital asset serves as a digital reflection of ownership and provides a level of transparency into the cap table of each structured note, including how much each investor invested."
>
> Andy Wiederhorn, CEO of FAT Brands[12]

DBRS Morningstar Credit Ratings reviewed the creditworthiness of the FAT Brands deal, thus giving more credence to the endeavor. The blockchain allowed for important features that gave visibility to token's associated cash flows of royalty rate, external party fees, management fees, and other expenses. Thus, the funds that pertain to the various facets of the business can easily be monitored and evaluated in real-time. According to one of the consultants who helped structure the offering: "You'll see when the money came in, when it went out, and how that whole waterfall works. It's definitely the first rated securitization with a digital asset element, and we're using it the way it was intended: to provide that level of transparency." FAT Brands token bond issuance serves as a watershed event for corporate finance on the blockchain!

> "Blockchains digitally record information in a continuous manner and data is stored using distributed ledger technology (DLT). DLT decentralizes and encrypts the storage of information, making manipulation by third parties difficult, which ultimately reduces the potential for fraud."
>
> Excerpt from DBRS Morningstar's pre-sale report[13]

Fund Ownership Tokens – These tokens provide their holders with a claim to a share of a fund. Each token will represent a specific number of rights or percentages to that fund. While the exact terms of profits and distributions will be determined by the fund's investor documents, holders of these tokens have the ability to trade their ownership stakes subject to restrictions. By tokenizing a fund, the underlying investments can obtain capital and not be subject to redemptions prior to optimal times – while at the same time, investors can find liquidity should they choose to via sales to other investors.

Industry Trends: Unlocking Private Equity Fund Liquidity

In September 2019, iCap Equity partnered with security token issuance platform provider Harbor to enhance the liquidity of four real estate ventures. These funds included more than 1,100 investors who had allocated in excess of $100 million in assets to property developments in the Pacific Northwest of the United States. The portfolios included holdings in multi-family, mixed-use, single-family residences, light commercial, and condominium properties.

Prior to tokenization, iCap's funds had reached maturity. At that point in time, some investors were looking to cash out while some were happy with their returns and wanted to keep their investments in the funds longer. By choosing to go forward through the use of a security token, iCap was able to enhance liquidity options for its investors as well as to reduce the steep discounts that come when investors are looking to trade out of a position. The token wrapper also allowed for compliance rules and secure record transfers of ownership to be enforced behind the scenes. This example shows that security token usage in the private equity fund space can add value and flexibility to investments. By using blockchain technology, private equity investments may be unlocked, thus providing a feasible investment option for many, potentially leading to a greater allocation by investors toward this style of private equity investing.

> "Technology that provides more liquidity among alternative assets could be transformational."
>
> Michael Bradley, CEO Bradley Wealth[14]

> "iCap Equity is pioneering a more efficient and liquid model for real estate investment funds, where they can lock up capital without locking up investors."
>
> Josh Stein, CEO Harbor[14]

Employee Stock Options

Another exciting example that highlights the flexibility and incredible possibilities of security tokens would come in the form of an employee stock option plan token. Start-ups, private businesses, and public companies could offer tokens as an efficient way to manage their traditional stock option planning.

By digitizing the stock option process, corporations will have a better way to reward employees for performance and can allow key personnel to participate in the upside of a company's growth. As security tokens offer self-maintaining cap tables and seamless reporting, they reduce management's burden around recordkeeping and accounting. Through the use of computer programming, corporations should be able to streamline what is often a highly complicated and time-intensive endeavor.

This process not only benefits the employer, but the employee as well as it could potentially create the optionality for liquidity. Stock options are typically very difficult to trade and often an event such as an acquisition or other change in control must arise in order for the options to be exercised or monetized. With a token stock option plan, the ease of selling or cashing in on stock options is greatly facilitated.

Case Study: Fidelity Investments Center for Applied Technology

As a way to incentivize its employees for good performance and attendance of corporate events, Fidelity Investments has issued its "BBT" token. These tokens will be available only to Fidelity employees and be part of a closed-loop rewards system. Fidelity partnered with San Francisco–based TokenSoft to deploy this token that uses the ERC-1404 standard. Fidelity's creation of an internal token signifies just how committed it is to rewarding its employees through tokens, but it also illustrates their promise of educating their workforce on how digital assets work.

> "For employees, it's a real use case for restricted tokens and gives them an opportunity to get hands-on experience with tokens, wallets, and other blockchain technology to understand how it works and how we might apply this in other areas."

> Juri Bulovic, Blockchain Product Manager at Fidelity Investments Center for Applied Technology[15]

> "Our goal is to make digitally native assets, such as Bitcoin, more accessible to investors."

> Abigail Johnson, CEO of Fidelity Investments[15]

Chapter Summary

- Stablecoins are cryptocurrencies designed to have reduced volatility as their price is often linked to a stated "stable" asset or basket of assets. As stablecoins representing fiat currencies become more popular, users will be able to hold digital forms of euro, British pound, Hong Kong dollar, Japanese yen, and theoretically any other currency.
- Asset-backed tokens constitute the economic rights to real-world assets like commodities, art, real estate, or infrastructure projects. The assets that underlie the token can be held by a custodian, by the entity promoting the token, or in the form of a trust.
- Tokens can also be created to represent ownership in bonds, equities, funds, as well as a slew of additional asset classes.

CHAPTER 4

SECURITY TOKENS WILL MASSIVELY DISRUPT AND VASTLY IMPROVE MARKETS

- There are many trillions of dollars of assets globally in need of liquidity – this capital could be tapped into with the use of new blockchain technology.
- Security tokens create better trading solutions for their issuers and investors.
- Digitization will enable higher economic growth, broader audiences of investors, and more efficient capital formation.
- Security tokens will help create new investment classes, new business, models and more complex financial offerings.

> "Blockchain technology isn't just a more efficient way to settle securities. It will fundamentally change market structures, and maybe even the architecture of the Internet itself."
>
> Abigail Johnson, CEO Fidelity Investments[1]

Tokenization is the next major wave of innovation in the financial markets as this technology will facilitate transactions and create security tokens. This new phase will open up ways for leading-edge opportunities to obtain funding from new sources at faster speeds and cheaper prices. It will allow businesses, entrepreneurs, and everyday people to create and access investments that were once unattainable.

According to a study by Savills and McKinsey, roughly 60% of the world's assets are inaccessible because of traditional market infrastructure. The study cites "information asymmetry, high costs and large ticket sizes prevent access from many investors."[2] Security tokens allow for new investment ideas that may never have even been considered as securities. The added dimensions of digital technologies will enable the investment community to implement bold new ideas that will amaze and capture the imagination of investors globally. By embracing blockchain technology and security tokens, society will see major enhancements in the form of:

a. **New Opportunities for Economic Growth**
b. **Broader Audiences of Investors**
c. **More Efficient Capital Formation**

Let's take a look at each of these three enhancements in greater detail.

New Opportunities for Economic Growth

It is said that there are many trillions of dollars of assets globally in need of liquidity – such needed capital could be tapped into with the use of new blockchain technology.[3] Security tokens provide a broad array of new capabilities for businesses to utilize. Security tokens can help to provide access to this funding in the following ways:

New Investment Classes – Possibly the most disruptive feature of security tokens lies in their potential to create new kinds of tradable assets. The range of properties that could be represented by security tokens is enormous and the number of types and specific assets tokenization will allow society to invest in will expand dramatically. Through tokenization, assets both tangible and intangible will be bought and sold more efficiently in the marketplace. This would include assets like artwork, royalties for music or videos, carbon credits, sports franchises, individual pieces of real estate, and so much more. In the future, perhaps you will much more affordably and easily be able to own a piece of your favorite sports team, a Picasso original, or the commercial rights to Bob Marley's music. These possibilities are not far off!

Digital token systems will enable the market to form these new types of securities (Figure 4.1). Previously, fractionalization of these assets could not be sustained due to inefficiencies and high cost structures. The legal complexity around some of these assets can be cumbersome but smart contracts provide a way to represent their ownership and provide a mechanism to track and distribute their economic benefits. Security tokens also enable these assets to be subdivided and syndicated to a wide array of investors in a more cost-effective way.

New Business Models – Many new business models will be developed to serve and capitalize on the technological possibilities of security tokens. The design around assets and their ownership can reach new levels as a result of the additional features available through the digital wrapper. These breakthroughs expand the chances for creativity and innovation in the financial and business spaces.

As more assets become tokenized, global trade and communications will become less difficult. Because of their digital format, security tokens allow for all sorts of data to be added to them. What might we be able to do if we can add or embed information such as reviews, videos, images, and legal documents into each of these tokens?

FIGURE 4.1   Asset Tokenization

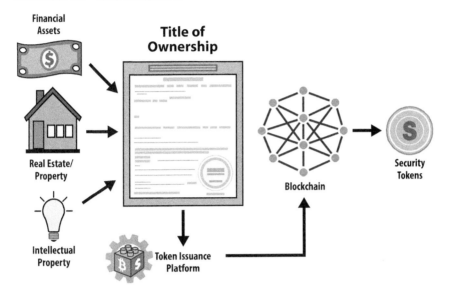

The breadth of options expands rapidly when viewed in this light. Token capabilities will expand way, way past what they are able to do now and will probably go so much farther than any of us today could envision!

If security tokens allow us to embed logic into the ownership title itself, we are forced to ask the question, "What else can we do?" As security tokens continue to gain initial adoption, we will likely see features taken to a new level and emboldened by imaginative individuals.

Digitization provides the ability to bring the underlying investment and its ownership closer together. Let's take the following hypothetical example:

Today, you can invest in the company that controls Marriott Hotels. What if in the future, ownership in shares of Marriott gave you the right to (A) a discount on a hotel room, (B) access to the VIP lounge, or (C) free meals at one of Marriott's restaurants? What if option A was possible had you been an investor for more than 10 years? What if option B was available if you owned over $100,000 worth of the shares? What if option C was available if you referred a friend to buy stock? In theory, all are possible with security tokens in a much cheaper, more timely and efficient way than could be done under the current financial regime.

More Complex Products – Some investors are looking for more sophisticated products than may be acquired in today's marketplace. Tokens provide increased flexibility in the structuring, designing, and strategizing of the shares themselves. With the use of smart contracts and digital offerings, there is the potential to create all sorts of situations to build a wide range of complex financial products. Coding will allow for mechanisms to deal with issues like contract breaches, credit enforcement, and legal disputes.

Tokens can be created to act in place of financial derivatives, insurance contracts, crowdfunding agreements, and even designed to deal with combinations of multiple factors. Today, one of the most commonly used products that employs the use of security tokens comes in the form of revenue share contracts. Businesses that rely on revenue percentages for royalties, mineral rights, real estate contracts, or key employee compensation agreements have turned to security tokens to create a more seamless solution to deal with cash flows.

Broader Audience of Investors

One of the tremendous advantages about security tokens comes in their ability to give direct access to individual investors and institutions. Both promoters and investors can reach one another at a far more rapid pace than today under our current regime. Security tokens will one day trade globally and this will make it so that anyone with access to the internet and within the appropriate regulatory limits can participate in a wide array of new economic opportunities. Today, there are many barriers that prevent that from happening in an efficient and timely way.

The decentralized trading structure for security tokens will enable the markets to open up to the widest possible pool of global capital. This will create new investment opportunities and reduce capital frictions in fundraising, investment, and value transfers.

New Investors – The potential for a larger investment base is created through the use of security tokens. Investments will soon be available to anyone with an internet connection and this exposure creates the opportunity for increases in asset valuations and the options by which people diversify their investment holdings.

In the past, high-priced assets were often only available to a select group of high-net-
worth investors. Projects that were once only presented to venture capital groups or private equity firms in their early stages of development may now very well be accessible through crowdfunding or other means over the internet. This will give anyone who is interested the chance to jump at investment opportunities they are excited about and provide the possibility of an immense amount of value creation should the endeavor turn into a success.

Security tokens also will likely bring new individuals into the world of investing. Those who have not participated in the capital markets before will no longer be burdened by factors such as not having a computer or stock brokerage account. Many individuals in emerging markets and lesser developed countries will be empowered by simply having mobile devices. This new breadth of reach could help to lessen poverty and increase savings rates around the world.

New Geographies – Today's investment opportunities lack exposure to a global shareholder base. Having been a portfolio manager for an internationally focused mutual fund strategy that catered to US investors, I can tell you firsthand from my many years of experience just how little some Americans invest overseas. The same is true for people who live outside the United States. This reluctance to put money in other areas of the world is commonly referred to as the "home country bias." Some studies have shown that until an individual has substantial cash assets, his or her abilities to put the money outside of the home country will be limited. Security tokens are a game changer from this perspective.

The standards under which security tokens operate will become more uniform, such that investing across regions will be much easier and investors will be able to buy and exchange tokens globally. Code can be written so cross-border regulatory standards may be met. Suppose a Dutch buyer is dealing with an American seller. The security token's embedded compliance protocols can ensure that rules mandated in the Netherlands are followed for the acquirer and that US rules are followed for the seller. If anything fails in the interim and some sort of rule can't be cleared, the blockchain won't allow the transaction to take place. Issuers of securities will be delighted to broaden their offerings from only US-accredited investors or eligible institutions to a potential of everyone throughout the world!

On top of all this, the bias that keeps people investing only in their home country or areas close to where they live can create a significant mispricing of assets. Security tokens will enable better free-market mechanisms and thus could lead to meaningful changes and equalizations of asset values globally. Capital should be able to flow more freely and thus properties should better reflect their true worth.

New Ways to Connect – With the advent of digital identity and the widespread use of mobile devices and mobile apps, securities can be traded in a compliant-friendly way at just about anyone's fingertips. Not only will investors be able to trade securities and issuers be able to broaden their reach, but also, the abilities to communicate on a global scale will be enhanced and be possible within a second's notice.

Issuers will have a more direct line of communication with their end investors. The list of owners and each one's respective stake in the holding will be accurate to the minute. Typical investor relations materials such as annual reports, management letters to shareholders, tax forms, or regulatory filings could be disseminated swiftly and easily as ownership is clear. Token owners will have their digital identities linked to their accounts and this will provide the correct avenues where information should be sent.

More Efficient Capital Formation

The enhancements brought forth by security tokens will facilitate the formation of capital for projects. By simplifying the ways in which liquidity can be unlocked, the project's uncertainty around funding is reduced and this lowers the cost of capital. On top of that, security tokens allow for certain costs to be stripped out of the equation both at issuance as well as in the subsequent trading in secondary markets. Projects and funds that choose to digitalize their offerings will stand out in the marketplace. The end consumer of the security tokens will be left with a better deal and enhanced capabilities. Here are a few of the reasons why capital markets will become more efficient with the use of security tokens:

Middlemen Removed – In today's financial world, intermediaries provide value in establishing safeguards to ensure compliance with regulatory standards. But if these services can be replaced by automating through the blockchain, their appeal (and cost!) would disappear. Security tokens will help to create frictionless processes and final customers will end up paying less for their investments.

Smart contracts embedded in the securities will reduce the paperwork and complexity that comes along with the issuing, transferring, and maintaining of a security. As these technologies speed up execution times, the attractiveness of the investment inevitably increases.

Lower Costs of Maintaining A Security Over Its Life Cycle – Managing a security over time can be painstaking and challenging to its issuer. Security tokenization will be a welcomed improvement to alleviate some of these problems.

The issuer of a new security will find it far easier to manage the endeavor's capital structure with the use of a security token. The capitalization table, or **cap table**, is a register that provides an analysis of a company's ownership stakes. Companies will often raise money at various stages – they will typically start off with initial investors, angel investors, and venture capitalists; investment bankers will usually come in at a later junction once a company has matured from a startup entity. Along the way, management may have needed to cut deals potentially involving equity dilutions, employee stock options, warrants, or other creative financing techniques. After several rounds of financing, a cap table can become quite complex.

Security tokens make this process simpler. As all of the inputs to this cap table can be automated and electronically tracked when an offering is digitized, the record-keeping tasks around ownership are streamlined. This will allow management to see a very accurate representation of who actually owns stakes in their companies and will provide a far clearer economic picture of how the company is doing on a fully diluted basis. The distributed ledger technology will automatically update this information in real time and prevent mistakes from occurring. This will enable better decision making and faster, cheaper corporate actions around the security.

Security tokens also provide more efficient and transparent payments of distributions to stakeholders. In today's marketplace, the costs around disbursing funds for dividends and debt servicing payments are enormous and will become somewhat irrational as better options exist through blockchain solutions. Why continue to mail checks or pay for third-party financial services to do a job when a security token can take care of that for you at a fraction of the price? It is not uncommon to see instances where the amount a shareholder is paid is lower than the cost to make the payment. Suppose you have a shareholder who owns roughly $100 worth of stock in a company and the quarterly dividend payment to that investor is 25 cents. An envelope and a stamp are maybe worth more than what he ends up receiving. Electronic payment with stablecoins is most certainly the better way to go if for no other reason than cost savings! By digitizing ownership, the transfer of assets between parties becomes about as easy as sending an email.

Better Governance Potential – Investors will often choose to invest in opportunities where governance and transparency are best. And to investors, hearing about good governance practices and the ability to witness good governance are two different things! The technology around security tokens will permit the investment community to access, test, and verify information in a quicker, cheaper, and more reliable way than ever before imagined.

For example, smart contracts could be used to continually monitor a company's debt covenants. Most lenders require a borrower to adhere to certain covenants and financial conditions such as maintaining a liquidity ratio above a stated level or not to exceed a certain borrowing limit. As smart contracts can be created to prevent and inform relevant parties when these kinds of caps are breached or are at a level that is near breach, creditors could be alerted that the debtor is not adhering to agreed-upon obligations or is close to violating agreed-upon limits. Smart contracts could also be written to divert funds to appropriate escrow accounts to see that debt obligations are met before other stakeholders receive those same funds.

With better governance potential, projects financed with security tokens should see a larger investor base and enjoy lower financing costs.

Industry Trends: Lowering the Cost of Money Transfers

According to the World Bank, the international market for remittances to low- and middle-income countries will be approximately $550 billion in 2019. A remittance payment is a transfer of money by a foreign worker to an individual in his or her homeland. These transactions usually occur when a worker in a foreign country is sending wages back to a family member or significant other in the native country. This is very common for foreign workers in places like the United States, the UK, Hong Kong, and the Middle East. Workers typically send money to countries such as the Philippines, Pakistan, Nigeria, or Mexico. Companies like Western Union, TransferWise, MoneyGram, Remitly, and Finablr assist with these cross-border transactions – albeit at a very high price to the transferring consumer. The fees can easily be in excess of 10% of the amount transferred; this takes a huge bite out of the worker's paycheck and often consumes a significant amount of time for both the sender and receiver.

Through the use of blockchain-based mobile apps, consumers have been able to find faster, cheaper, and more transparent solutions when sending money back to their loved ones and family abroad. With blockchain, payments are sent directly from person to person without going through an intermediary. Companies such as Abra and Bitspark transfer payments for as little as just a few cents. They also offer multiple access points for remittance receivers to collect their cash at kiosks and retail outlets in the home country. In the end, blockchain enables workers to keep more of their hard-earned money.

"Our current financial system relies largely on wire transfers, which are backed by traditional banks and other financial institutions. It's a reasonably good system, but one of the problems with it is that it takes time to process transactions. Blockchain-based mobile payment systems companies can outmaneuver traditional wire transfer companies by offering a fast, cheap, and secure system to transfer money from one part of the world to another."

Kevin Rands, Founder of the Disruptor Daily[4]

"The ubiquitous proliferation of mobile devices and enhancements in tele-density is now enabling customers to demand services not just on their doorsteps but from the comfort of their living rooms. ... Blockchain will introduce a new era of disintermediation leading to openness, decentralization, and global inclusion that will give us unprecedented capabilities of efficiently creating and trading value in society."

Tariq Bajwa, Governor of the State Bank of Pakistan[4]

The case of remittance payments demonstrates the rapid and intrusive potential of blockchain. It shows how the technology can quickly reach the farthest corners of the earth and affect all levels of society. It witnesses how new business can sprout and shake the cage of age-old firms that act as intermediaries. And it validates how costs and transaction times can be lessened. Many other financial lines of business will likely see the same fate.

To Tokenize or Not to Tokenize?

While it is certainly possible for just about any asset to be tokenized, security issuers will need to decide for themselves if their needs are being best met by choosing to go down the route of offering a security token. There are certain industries and asset classes whose fundamentals are inherently more well suited to blockchain solutions. In the end, though, one must ask the question, "What am I really getting out of tokenizing this asset and does the cost outweigh the benefits?"

The digital revolution has the potential to enhance offerings, lower costs, and improve efficiency; but some of those benefits, while realistic, are not yet achievable at this time. It may be a few more years before all of the game-changing aspects of security tokens are commonplace in the market. As a result, only offerings that have the utmost to gain from tokenizing will do so for now. Other assets will wait until the technology and cost structure are better. For tokens to really derive value, end users must feel they are getting something from the tokenized platform that is not available from traditional avenues.

Chapter Summary

- By embracing blockchain technology and security tokens, society will see major benefits. This includes new opportunities for economic growth, broader communities of investors, and more efficient capital formation.
- There are many trillions of dollars of assets globally in need of liquidity – this capital could be tapped into with the use of new blockchain technology. Security tokens provide an option to create better trading solutions for their issuers and investors.
- Security tokens will help create new investment classes, new business models, and more complex financial offerings.
- Tokens will broaden the geographies and demographics of investors for certain projects.
- Tokenization will lower the cost of maintaining a security over its lifespan. Tokens enhance potential for better corporate governance and transparency for investors.
- For tokens to really deliver value, the end-users must feel they are getting worthwhile features from the tokenized platforms that are not available from traditional avenues.

PART II

CREATING THE DIGITAL WRAPPER

CHAPTER 5

KEY FEATURES OF A SECURITY TOKEN

- Security tokens should be designed to deal with issues that will likely occur throughout their lifecycle.
- Know Your Customer (KYC) and Anti-Money-Laundering (AML) provisions can be handled more efficiently through the use of tokens.
- Security tokens can reduce costs over the long haul for both issuers and investors.
- Security tokens offer the ability for enhanced safety and heightened transparency.

Security tokens are creating excitement in the financial industry as these tokens combine the best of the latest technology and the potential for world-class investor protections, regulatory compliance, and customer service. In order to deliver a heightened user experience and enhanced economics, security tokens will need to contain certain functionality and capabilities. This section of the book covers the necessary building blocks of a security token.

Security Administration

There are many stages and activities critical in the administration of a security. To ensure the safety, soundness, and risk mitigation of a security in the financial marketplace, tokens should be designed to handle the aspects of administration in a robust, orderly, and automated fashion.

Tokens should be created to deal with a number of issues, including the following:

- Issuance and redemption
- Security transfers
- Risk mitigation
- Distributions of payments, splits, tenders, or other corporate actions
- Stakeholder voting

- Investor relations and communications
- Tax withholdings
- Net asset value calculations
- Regulatory compliance and reporting

Tokenization automates, standardizes, streamlines, and provides transparency to many of these processes, thus protecting and mitigating risk for both issuers and investors. A well-designed security token should have many of the features and capabilities to handle much of these administrative duties.

Compliance

Regulatory agencies around the world require that issuers of securities take steps to ensure all necessary laws and procedures are followed when issuing a security. Safeguards have to be put in place to ensure the security and its owners remain in compliance over time. This is a cumbersome burden for promoters to bear but fortunately, protocols may be embedded into a security token to maintain regulatory compliance and avoid illegal activities.

Maintaining compliance with security laws is a huge cost for both publicly and privately traded assets. Security issuers are held responsible by government entities to make sure their assets remain in-line with the law. Cross-border settlement treatments, investor accreditation verification, anti-money-laundering provisions, and maintaining internal guidelines are just a few examples of the responsibilities that managers of these assets face. Fortunately, security tokens provide mechanisms to automate compliance procedures. This feature reduces the onus of these requirements and makes security tokens appealing to both issuers and investors.

Compliance processes can be embedded directly into the security itself through token standards or smart contracts whenever a new token is issued, stripping out costs that can be experienced in markets relying on traditional paper-form securities. Through automation, anytime a token is transferred to or from an existing account, a compliance engine will be called upon to ensure the transaction meets the necessary requirements before it changes hands. A series of trade conditions are monitored and if any steps fail, the entire order will not go through onto the blockchain as the system stops itself. This self-enforcement mechanism enables one to easily determine whether a party involved in the trade is compliant or if more information is needed. This creates a structured, scalable solution that brings down fees and reduces the amount of time needed to consummate a valid transaction.

By substituting code in exchange for middlemen, a security issuer is able to meet all regulatory rules and the risks of government interference are more or less removed. Bad actors will be avoided and trades will be executed in a manner that provides assurance of proper compliance. By reducing the uncertainty, investors will have more confidence in what they are buying.

Companies specializing in compliance can update the token's procedures as regulatory rules change and improvements can be seamlessly added as they become available. By having a compliance system that is interoperable with the rest of the token features, securities will be in observance of all relevant regulations and internal policy standards.

KYC & AML

In terms of regulations, it is vital for an issuer to know the following:

Who is buying the asset? How did they learn about the project? In what jurisdiction does he or she reside? When did they purchase the asset?

Procedures such as Know Your Customer (KYC) and Anti-Money-Laundering (AML) are two of the most important regulatory aspects for a security issuer to consider. Both are legally required before any investor takes a financial interest in a security.

Investors want to go through these onboarding processes in a manner that is as simple and frictionless as possible. In today's marketplace, if an investor wants to purchase assets from multiple firms, he or she will have to provide the necessary personal information time and time again as each vendor will have to go through its own series of onboarding investigations. For example, if someone wanted to open bank accounts with HSBC and with Bank of America, practically the exact same paperwork would have to be completed on both occasions. On top of that, two separate compliance officers would be reviewing the same documents and information, thus resulting in undue costs and unnecessarily long processing times. This situation creates the potential for compromised information that is less secure than need be.

By using blockchains and digital identities, the market now has the potential to transform this outdated process of storing information so that it can be referenced on an ongoing basis. Security token users will obtain more control over their personal information and will be verified through automated standards. This will lower the administrative burden of many securities to which we have grown accustomed.

By using blockchain-based protocols to check real-world identities, heavy-duty due diligence of investors is performed quickly and inexpensively. Software verifies that a specific wallet address corresponds to a particular person or entity in real time. Steps are taken to look for sanctioned individuals or countries, foreign ownership limits, maximum numbers of investors, multiplicity of wallets, and other factors. This will easily determine whether the party buying or selling a security token is compliant or if additional screening and information is necessary.

Accounting and Reporting

Digital platforms will allow for automated reporting and analytics generation as well as the full dissemination of financial statements to shareholders and regulators. Tokenization also creates a mechanism for better tracking and audit capabilities. Through digitalization, systems will be much more efficient than current manual processes; again, this saves users time and money while providing better accountability.

Security promoters work with service providers within the token ecosystem to make sure that transactions are done the right way at every turn. This will make reporting more auditworthy and create controls that are well tested and capable of providing reliable outputs. It will also allow the ledger to contain a rich log of trading, distributions, and other corporate actions' histories.

Security tokens will also enhance a project's investor relations capabilities. With electronic dissemination of information, communications can go out to all stake-holders at once with just a click of a button. Confirmation messages can be sent back to the issuer showing that messages have been received and read. Distributed ledger technology will also facilitate proper accounting for taxes and withholdings on all distributions. Expensive annual meetings could potentially be replaced through online voting and investor feedback.

Safety Mechanisms

Lost or Stolen Tokens – Properly constructed security tokens should offer the ability to reissue tokens to their rightful holders if necessary. There are many circumstances that could occur that would require the recovery or forced transfer of a token. For example, if a token holder died, his or her heirs would want to claim legal ownership. Just because the new beneficiary did not have the proper passwords to a wallet or the access to a security token, there is no good reason why this value should be stranded. Other considerations like law-enforcement actions, sanctions, or court-ordered settlements could necessitate the forceful transfer of a security token.

Cryptocurrencies are bearer assets; anyone can freely and anonymously acquire them. But if lost by means of hacking or inability to access a wallet, cryptos cannot be recovered and the investor will be at a complete loss. Security tokens on the other hand are registered and have validated investors with legally protected rights. So long as an investor fulfills the necessary legal requirements, he or she should have the right to reclaim tokens wrongfully removed from possession. Digital wallet providers and issuance platforms can assist investors who lose their wallet keys subject to terms and conditions.

Changes in Regulatory Environment – Should there be a failure in blockchain technology or some sort of regulatory shutdown, a token issuer will always have the ability to revert back to paper. It is important to remember a blockchain is simply a distributed ledger that records who owns an asset and the recorded aspects around that ownership. So, if something happens due to an unlikely event, you will always know what is owned and who owns it. Blockchain's ability to facilitate instant recordkeeping can help ensure that. As long as each token is properly linked to a compliant digital identity, there should not be a reason to fear the misappropriation of a security token.

Code Audits – Issuers, investors, and exchanges will need to see a token's programming code to verify its safety and robustness. Code auditing professionals will examine each line of computer code with the intent of discovering bugs, potential security breaches, or violations of proper conventions or protocols.

A code audit is a key step to reduce errors before the token is released. During the audit, each important component of the token's code will be inspected separately as well as in its entirety with the whole project. If a vulnerability is detected, its risk can be eliminated or mitigated before any problems need to be remedied.

Chapter Summary

- Security tokens should be designed to deal with issues that will likely occur throughout their lifecycle. This includes embedding features into the token itself to handle administration and compliance.
- Regulatory issues such as Know Your Customer (KYC) and Anti-Money-Laundering (AML) provisions can be handled more efficiently through the use of tokens.
- By containing certain features, security tokens can reduce costs over the long haul for both issuers and investors.
- Security tokens offer the ability for enhanced safety and heightened transparency.

CHAPTER 6

THE SECURITY TOKEN ECOSYSTEM

- An ecosystem of financial firms has been developed to support the ongoing usage of security tokens. Fintech companies are working to improve today's financial infrastructure.
- The token ecosystem consists of three main groups: protocols, issuance platforms, and advisory services.
- Blockchains must exhibit a high degree of interoperability for maximum efficiency.
- The token stack is the collection of interconnected layers of functionalities that ultimately define the capabilities and behavioral elements of a security token.

Fintech Companies

Some of the best and brightest from both the financial and technology community are working to develop the digital infrastructure that will dominate the securities markets of tomorrow. As security tokens gain momentum in the marketplace, a clear ecosystem of companies and projects that support the issuance, exchange, custody, compliance, and other services important for digital securities is beginning to form.

The blockchain space has now had over ten ten years of constant engineering and refinement to digitize processes, enable automation, and drive efficiency. A new group of entrepreneurial firms, referred to as **Fintechs**, has developed to simplify and improve how we interact with the money, assets, and investments we possess. One of the preferred ways these firms look to revolutionize the financial markets is through the use of blockchain. The creative individuals working in Fintech are putting in the time, effort, and energy to modernize the financial marketplace so it will work in a better way.

According to Kepler Finance, more than $600 million has been invested in firms that are developing the necessary applications to bring the digitization of assets mainstream.[1] This capital is being used to develop and test various solutions which will help to grow and mature the security token ecosystem from both a technical and regulatory perspective. By creating platforms that allow for embedded regulations and conform to the latest technological innovations, these cutting-edge firms are creating a path toward a sustainable transition away from the traditional methods by which securities are issued and transacted today.

In building the foundations for tomorrow's security markets, it is becoming clear that smart contracts will need a group of third-party facilitators to help access data and perform operations that are not suitable for the blockchain. The **token ecosystem** consists of all service providers that aid in the proper functioning of regulated digital assets. This would include protocols, issuance platforms, liquidity providers like exchanges, custodians, transfer agents and advisory services.

Protocols

Earlier we discussed how protocols played an important role in how blockchain technologies operate. As a recap, **protocols** are rules for electronic communication. Protocols should be open and well understood; when this is the case, they can become powerful tools to foster innovation and reduce costs. Strong protocols are the foundation for a system's interoperability.

Interoperability is one of the most significant benefits that will be obtained as we move toward a world of security tokens. **Interoperability** is the characteristic of a technological system where all hardware and software applications can readily exchange information and make use of the data they receive. It is critical for systems to have interoperability so that all processes can be run from end to end without error or disruption. When systems are interoperable, data becomes exceptionally mobile and the full benefits of multiple applications working together can be realized.

Take the example of how telephones work. It doesn't matter your brand of phone or whether the call you make is from a wireless or landline connection – if you make a call to someone, that person will be able to receive your signals and understand you. In turn, you will be able to understand whatever is sent your way. Your phone has the ability to talk to any other phone without having to go through custom developments or integrations to make that happen. Your phone can connect and interact with any other phone without needing to know any other details about that phone. That is a very powerful feature of the way our communications network is designed.

To develop a seamless digital security ecosystem, a combination of several elements must be working together to provide the full gamut of activities needed to administer a security over its entire life cycle. This includes being able to provide start-to-finish solutions for token issuance, regulatory compliance, legal validation, custody, trading, and other important actions. Tokens must be formatted correctly to work across the network of ecosystem players.

With many Fintech companies striving to develop new technologies, the question that must be asked is "Are these companies working together to produce interoperable solutions?" It is only once interoperability is ironed out that an asset will be able to move freely across markets and holders efficiently. Only then will security tokens provide their fullest benefits to society.

Token Standards   Interoperability is facilitated by the creation and use of standards. **Standards** define the rules by which tokens and the platforms on which they operate function. Standards include information about protocol specifications and contract descriptions. Common standards define how certain functions will behave and allow applications and smart contracts to interact with them in a predictable way. Standards are typically employed as established norms, or as requirements for a repeatable technical task. Blockchain standards are written around how to deal with digital identity, smart contract execution, token design, recurring transactions, and other important processes that are commonly relied upon in the community.

Developers and technicians in the Fintech community are incentivized to find common ground upon which to establish standards. Doing so can provide many economic benefits when certain protocols are regarded as the way to do business. Rather than everyone reinventing the wheel, a standard creates a network effect as the products that use it can attract a greater number of users. As a result, code is often shared for free within the blockchain community so that many will employ the same methods across multiple offerings to promote interoperability.

Cooperation can become difficult as more and more are involved, but it is at this time when establishing standards becomes more complex and more essential. By creating a common set of standards and clear protocols, blockchain applications obtain the ability to scale.

Although we cover regulation in another chapter, it is important to note that one of the biggest hurdles to reaching accepted standards and interoperability is due to the complexity of legal and compliance requirements that have not yet been clearly defined in the industry. Regulatory aspects often boil down to people and getting groups to reach a compromise or find common ground. Oftentimes, forging the cooperation of people is much harder than forging the cooperation of machines. This is why it may take a few more years before all of the amazing benefits of security tokens can be realized.

Ethereum ERC Standards   Up until this point in time, many in the Fintech industry have gravitated towards the Ethereum blockchain to shape the architecture for digital securities because of the Ethereum Request of Comments, or ERC, standards. The Ethereum blockchain contains ERC standards to be used with tokens that operate on the platform. These standards allow anybody to run a program, and make building a new application much less difficult. Developers do not have to start from scratch when forming a new piece of software nor are they bound to write code in any particular programming language. With ERCs, better user interfaces can be created as it is easy to adjoin wizards or oracles on top of smart contract applications. This provides an incredible amount of flexibility around Ethereum and is the reason why many advisory services have chosen this particular blockchain for security token issuance.

Ethereum already has several foundational standards in place and today, more ERCs are being proposed. The Ethereum community is reviewing the documents detailing what these suggested standards will accomplish and how they will be carried out. The community can then decide whether to accept the standards as a general way of doing things. As more and more standards are admitted as protocols, the likelihood of security tokens remaining in compliance and being interoperable will be virtually guaranteed and the general ideas behind these standards could potentially be applied on other chains.

Today, Ethereum is the most established blockchain for security tokens. Ethereum's safe and proven mechanisms for handling smart contracts and its ERC standards have made it a go-to place for digital offerings. Over time, though, we have seen other distributed ledger technology solutions like Tezos, Algorand, Hyperledger and Hedera Hashgraph attract development and new business. Some would say this is because the technology behind Ethereum is lacking when placed head-to-head against new entrants. In particular, questions around Ethereum's speed, transaction costs and scalability will need to be resolved in order for it to remain in a leading position. Only time will tell if Ethereum can maintain its dominant market share.

Issuance Platforms

Issuance platforms are consulting organizations that assist projects that want to tokenize their ownership. Promoters generally do not have the adequate knowledge around the technical or regulatory requirements needed to issue a digital security. The issuance platforms make these matters much more straightforward and reduce the time and know-how needed to take a security token to market by bringing everything together under one roof.

Issuance platforms assist in the token's design, the creation of smart contracts, and provide a user interface for investor prospects to register and send the project money. The role of these platforms extends well beyond facilitating the appropriate technical solution. Some platforms manage not only the issuance of a token but also the entire life cycle of the token. This includes services such as custody, anti-money-laundering checks, compliance, transfer agency functions, and corporate actions. Issuance platforms can also provide assistance when a token is lost or inaccessible to a token holder. In short, issuance platforms are vital for the successful launching of security tokens that are fully compliant with all government regulations.

Issuance platforms contribute to the efficient launching of a security token. They help projects to facilitate record keeping and integrate the processes that are utilized by various data intermediaries. This enhances the ease of use of tokens and helps to mitigate risks.

Issuance platforms often differ in that each platform may focus on a specific technology, geographical area, or industry. These platforms may also use blockchain technologies differently. One firm may have expertise in Ethereum, another in Tezos or Hedera Hashgraph. Some may use one set of standards while others may choose a different route altogether. Some may use in-house solutions while others will advise the use of third-party providers. The specialization of the issuance platform needs to be carefully considered in order to be sure not only that technical specifications are handled best but also that all the specific compliance requirements and data protection laws pertaining to the security token are met.

Advisory Services

Third-party services will be needed as security token markets continue to develop. By utilizing the services of outsourced professionals, token issuers and investors will find ways to reduce the risks in making these offerings and acquire necessary perspectives and tools to best grow the business in a sustainable way. While the list of categories for advisory services could be quite extensive, below are three of the most relevant.

Law Firms   The first, and probably most important, step for any issuer or investor to successfully get involved in digital securities is to make sure everything they are doing is on proper legal footing. Laws can be extremely complicated in issuing, trading, and dealing with financial instruments such as securities. It is highly advisable to consult a qualified lawyer before dealing with any security tokens.

Generally speaking, security tokens are regarded the same as traditional securities. Just because the wrapper around the security is now digital does not mean the rules have changed. Many promoters have gotten into trouble by making this mistake. When looking for a lawyer, it is best to go with someone who understands the technology and the ecosystem around the security token business.

As blockchain and other automating technologies are coming to the forefront, legal professionals specializing in securities law will need to obtain some level of technical training in order to stay relevant. Law firms are starting to employ more personnel who have the technical competence necessary to structure security tokens, evaluate smart contracts, and administer the proper legal frameworks around deals. Over time, the legal documentation pertinent to security tokens will likely become more standardized. Many legal elements will eventually become embedded into the securities themselves rather than being recorded on paper as was done in yesteryears.

Custodians   **Custodians** provide safeguarding of a firm's, fund's, or individual's assets. These institutions are typically not engaged in traditional financial services such as retail banking or mortgage lending. Custodians will hold the actual assets, whether stocks, fixed income instruments, or precious metals. The custodians can provide services around these assets such as arranging settlement around transactions, performing tax and accounting work, or administrating corporate actions.

Custodians play an important role in the financial markets. Certain institutions, like mutual funds and pension funds, are legally required to house their holdings with a custody bank. Laws have been put in place to ensure the beneficiaries of these plans will be the ones to eventually receive the assets behind them. Custody banks and the use thereof theoretically prevent bad actors from absconding with any monies.

Today, there seems to be increasing appetite for trusted and qualified traditional custodians with the ability to service and hold nontraditional assets, namely digital assets. Clients are looking for established custodians as this could increase comfort and credibility and help to satisfy legal requirements for institutions starting to get involved in the digital space.

The issue around proper custody is a tricky one and has caused a lot of friction with regulators who are keen on keeping assets and investors safe. As certain digital assets, in particular cryptocurrencies, have limited, if any, regulation and there is little means to unwind trades, defining what is "custody" can be fairly difficult. Global regulators have yet to provide a formal framework to address how digital assets must be handled. It is this lack of clarity and the potential for alterations in current legal standards that put existing custodians in a particularly challenging position. As a result, larger custody firms have tended to shy away from the digital space and are waiting to see how things evolve before dipping into the market. Smaller firms, on the other hand, have the opportunity to jump in the market with a first mover advantage.

Validators   In order to meet regulatory and compliance standards, a token will have to undergo certain checks every time value is transferred. Whenever there is a request to trade a token, the blockchain will need to know if all end-users are authenticated and legally capable of taking part in an exchange. **Validators** are services that provide mechanisms to verify digital identities, perform Know Your Customer (KYC) and Anti-Money-Laundering (AML) assessments, and assure that ongoing compliance standards are met. Validators confirm that all participants have the proper credentials to trade and transact. This reduces the risks and time it takes to consummate a legitimate transaction.

Validators will be needed not only for issuance and trading but also for times when corporate actions are made. If a company that backs a token issues a dividend, validators may need to ensure certain facts such as if the recipient is still legally eligible to receive funds or that proper tax reporting information is up to date.

Validators can also be used as an important means to ensure privacy. A token holder may be willing to provide her identity to acquire property but likely will not want her personal information disseminated any further. Validators can safeguard information and use the blockchain in a way that maintains discretion while simultaneously delivering a compliant method for providing sensitive information.

The Token Stack: Putting It All Together

If designed properly, a security token has the potential to bring its issuers and investors massive efficiencies, reduced risk, and the connection to a global pool of liquidity. The **token stack** is the collection of interconnected layers of functionality that ultimately define the capabilities and behavioral elements of a security token. In order to be a high-quality product, a security token must follow all regulations and offer many of the exciting features made possible through blockchain technology. (See Figure 6.1.)

A typical token stack contains four layers: blockchain, token standards, validator systems, and liquidity providers. While the layers of the token stack each have their own distinct purposes and functions, the services each perform can be gathered through a combination of different Fintech firms in the token ecosystem. As discussed earlier, the issuance platform might supply multiple amenities and thus be an integral part of several layers of a stack. Then again, a token stack may also consist of a multitude of suppliers each providing a unique functionality critical to the success of the token.

For a security token to operate at a high level, it needs to:

- Be built on a blockchain that is scalable and tested for the particular environment in which it is intended to operate
- Possess interoperable features that are seamless from end to end
- Remain compliant at all times
- Be capable of handling all lifecycle management requirements
- Provide sufficient liquidity in a reliable, cost-effective manner

FIGURE 6.1   Token Stack Illustration

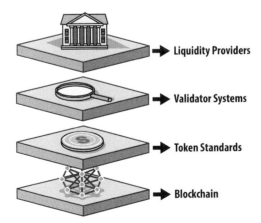

Liquidity Providers

Validator Systems

Token Standards

Blockchain

Chapter Summary

- An ecosystem of financial firms has been developed to support the ongoing usage of security tokens.
- Fintech companies are working to better today's current financial infrastructure.
- The token ecosystem consists of three main groups: protocols, issuance platforms, and advisory services.
- In order for tokens to be as beneficial to society as possible, the technologies being developed must exhibit a high degree of interoperability.
- At this time, Ethereum has the largest community of security tokens because of its ability to run widely accepted standard protocols.
- Issuance platforms are consulting organizations that assist projects that want to tokenize their ownership.
- Advisory services are third-party firms that facilitate many important supplemental functions for tokens.
- The token stack is the collection of interconnected layers of functionalities that ultimately define the capabilities and behavioral elements of a security token.

PART **III**

REALIZING THE POTENTIAL OF SECURITY TOKENS

CHAPTER 7

REGULATION OF DIGITAL ASSETS

- In order to achieve broader acceptance, security tokens will need to embrace regulation and best compliance practices.
- Uncertainties around regulation are one of the biggest challenges hindering the development of security tokens for the broader public.
- Countries around the world view security tokens with a wide array of opinions.

A Regulatory View From 50,000 Feet

Issuing securities brings about certain regulatory requirements. The principal obstacle standing in the way of widespread security token adoption comes in the form of regulation. One of the greatest challenges around security tokens today is how to place the near limitless potentials of the blockchain within the necessary legal frameworks. Regulation is an incredibly complex and evolving topic; there are numerous regulators across different jurisdictions and in some cases, multiple regulators in the same jurisdiction. Unfortunately, the technology around tokens has been developed far faster than have the legal parameters within which they operate.

In order for security tokens to thrive and successfully achieve mass adoption in the marketplace, the public will need to perceive them as stable, efficient, and safe. As a result, digital assets and their issuers will need to adhere to regulatory, compliance, and money transfer laws. They will need to meet these common standards and have reliable customer protections. Adhering to the rules will provide a token with the legal footing needed to be successful over the long run. Only then will authorities provide the green light for more frequent offerings to a wider array of investors.

Unfortunately, society's perception of blockchain assets is unnecessarily negative due to certain nefarious encounters with the technology. Cryptocurrencies are regarded as risky and uncertain speculative propositions; and for good or bad, all digital assets have been lumped together with this group in the general public's mindset. Bitcoin and many of its alternatives were deliberately designed to be unregulated, operating without any formal government filings or investor safeguards. These cryptocurrencies were successful in that they made the transferring of their ownership far simpler and efficient in a technical sense; but they also exhibited a downside. In the absence of any normal protections, token purchasers often found themselves the victims of scams, cyber-hacks, or pyramid schemes. The website coinschedule.com has stated that cryptocurrencies and utility tokens have cumulatively raised over $20 billion through the end of 2018.[1] It's no wonder that people are skeptical: many have invested quite a bit of money and been left with little or nothing to show for it.

Many people who invested in crypto were quite aware of the risks they were taking. There were those who liked the fact that little could be done to interfere in the marketplace and some actually saw it as a benefit that the governments' hands would be tied from doing anything. Others accepted that by investing in this market, they might never again see their money and realized the speculative nature of their investment. But then, there were a lot of players who came to the cryptocurrency game with no idea or understanding of what they were doing. They had no comprehension of how the laws of supply and demand governed markets or how speculative manias worked. Several promoters came along who were merely scammers and looked to exploit these types of unsophisticated investors.

It should come as no surprise that regulators eventually intervened to protect their citizenry. In most cases, regulators warned that all tokens were subject to the same laws and regulations as traditional financial instruments. The authorities made it clear that just because cutting-edge blockchain technology was involved, by no means would they tolerate having the existing legal precedents and regulations thrown out the window. The seedy underbelly of the crypto world was put on notice and some bad actors were disciplined. The actions of the regulators worked and they began to clean up the space.

As it became clear that blockchain could provide more than just crypto or utility functionality, regulators realized the need to develop guidelines under which security tokens and all digital assets could function. In turn, statements, rulings, opinions, and procedures were laid out to give clarity as to what was and was not acceptable. Governing bodies realized the awesome power blockchain held – they had to be careful not to be so slow and restrictive as to smother the potential of this new technology; yet at the same time, the regulators couldn't give free reign and let the situation move beyond their control. As a result, the public had to adopt a wait-and-see attitude as to the regulators' next move.

Throughout the course of history, laws and regulations have struggled to keep up with new disruptive innovations. As rules develop to govern how security tokens operate, local authorities and customs will dominate the way transactions unfold.

Politicians at the federal or local level will end up determining how security tokens will function and there will be no way to generalize just how regulations will work at a universal level with 100% certainty. As such, local jurisdictions will play a critical role in determining the specific regulations that pertain to each security token.

Security tokens will be the next evolution of digitalization as they combine the speed and agility of blockchain with the regulation standards needed to function in an efficient marketplace. By incorporating the appropriate mechanisms to remain compliant, security tokens can be developed in a way that takes us forward legally and ultimately, regulation is good for token holders. With strong mechanisms in place to safeguard the investor, people will be less fearful about losing their money through scams or wrongful means. Instead, investors will shift their concerns where they are supposed to be – as to whether the economic success of the underlying assets is realized!

How Regulators Might Respond

Regulatory authorities are starting to understand the advantages of global security token standards and thus will want to support their implementations. Those ventures taking advantage of the technology behind the security tokens and issuing such tokens in connection with projects or other assets desperately need a regulatory environment that provides less ambiguity than what we are seeing today. As these developments unfold, the market will begin to understand the relevant regulations that apply, the context under which they fall, and how compliance is accomplished. Once this clarity is assured, security tokens can be created with the correct rules applied so that the steps necessary to enforce those rules can be algorithmically coded.

Digitization increases a regulator's ability to perform effective oversight as transparency and reliability are so much greater. Security tokens help to enforce regulations in that they enhance the security's own ability to police itself and report to all what has transpired. In this type of environment, regulatory authorities will be able to apply more control and more compliance standards rather than less. On top of that, regulators will have the tools to be more proactive rather than spending needless time simply being reactive. This situation will place regulators in a stronger position to better control transgressions in the market and allow legislative goals to be better met. As a result, regulators will accept security tokens because of their incredible potential to deliver benefits not only to investors but also to governmental authorities and the regulators themselves. Perhaps there will come a time when regulators require the digitization of securities!

We seem to be on the edge of a virtuous circle where more and more understanding between regulators, the public, and security issuers and sponsors is being developed. We are simultaneously gaining legal certainty and the technology being developed to match what is needed to take security token issuance to the next level of acceptance and utilization.

Jurisdictions

Ideally the market for security tokens would be borderless, but that doesn't mean that the security laws in local jurisdictions where the issuers, projects, and holders reside can be avoided. Issuers of security tokens and other digital assets must be very careful where they choose to do business and raise funds for their projects in appropriate and regulation-friendly jurisdictions. Promoters will seek out locations whose regulators have a reputation for meeting high international standards but are not so restrictive that innovation and investment are choked off with overly expensive, cumbersome, or unnecessary rules. As is the case in all markets, those jurisdictions that provide clarity, simplicity, expediency, and follow-through will lure businesses while those that add hassle and uncertainty will impede development.

Countries know they have to compete for business especially when it comes to attracting industries with the potential for high productivity or growth. As a result, some nations are establishing friendly regulatory environments to attract and poach talent from other jurisdictions in the security token industry. As the financial marketplace continues it's path toward digitization, much is likely to be gained by the nations that position themselves near the center of this technological revolution.

The jurisdiction within which a project selects to be domiciled is a major decision that will have long-term ramifications for success. Choosing the right jurisdiction in which to incorporate can be advantageous in terms of cost, speed, reputation, tax advantages, and/or freedoms to make choices. In order to decide about a jurisdiction, much research has to be undertaken and legal and tax experts should be consulted.

Countries at the Forefront of Adoption

There are a select few jurisdictions in the world that have been working to embrace distributed ledger technology as they realize its potential to create employment and prosperity. Nations that cultivate the ecosystem around security tokens will likely see an influx of wealth, job creation, and synergistic economic advancement. Trends show though that smaller, less populated countries are moving faster toward digital development, most likely due to the dynamics and structure of their economies. Their nimble and quick forward-thinking actions could prove to pay big dividends for their economies in the years to come. In larger, more developed economies, it will take a lot of new jobs and activity to move the needle on growth. While digital adoption can certainly drive efficiency and productivity, the magnitude of the boom in growth would be relatively more meaningful for a small nation than for China or Germany or the United States. On top of that, digital securities inevitably bring with them an element of political risk – low-level jobs in finance could be eliminated, existing businesses may be overtaken, or legislation may be too lax for some. As a result, the risk–reward trade-off is such that developed countries may remain on the sidelines and let others take the lead.

In some smaller countries, it may be easier and more convenient for the regulators and those employed in the security token industry to work together. Security token participants and pioneers may be more likely to have a greater voice with regulators in these markets. Regulators and members of the financial community will likely begin to compromise with one another so as to create a solution that is beneficial to the country as a whole.

Places where the government wants to grow its jurisdiction's standing by holding itself out as "digital friendly" are likely to see groundbreaking developments and experimentation in the digital asset space. Other nations will look to these countries who are at the forefront for guidance. Adoption by the countries who at first took a "wait and see" attitude will start to take hold once those nations who took the "take the bull by the horns" approach refine and time-test their newly developed processes and procedures.

Switzerland Switzerland has long been regarded as one of the safest countries in the world to do business. Not only does Switzerland provide investors with world-class services but it is also renowned for the legal protections it offers. Switzerland's FINMA has delineated definitions for digital assets and provided guidance clarifying how tokens should be issued. Also, the country's taxing authority has made rulings that allow security tokens to enjoy the same exemptions from profit and value-added assessments as would happen when raising standard capital.

The country's premier exchange, SIX, has heavily invested in creating a trading platform to handle security tokens in a nationally regulated way. SIX's director, Thomas Zeeb, announced that it would be preferable to tokenize existing securities, including equities, fixed income, and funds. The Swiss government has also announced a strategy that recognizes DLT as an important development in the financial services sector; as a result, there are plans to lay further regulatory groundwork in the coming months.[3] These and other features are key reasons why Switzerland will likely be a critical country for the development of security tokens in the future.

Malta The Mediterranean island nation of Malta has made clear signals of its intention to be a go-to destination for firms looking to develop the security token ecosystem. Dubbed "Blockchain Island," Malta has passed a plethora of laws to provide a clear framework upon which companies can build the infrastructure needed to issue, manage, and service security tokens. Both regulators and politicians seem to be on board with this initiative. The Prime Minister of Malta recently spoke at a conference held in the capital city of Valletta and articulated his vision for why his country wanted to be at the forefront of tokenization.[2]

Part of Malta's allure comes from the fact that it is part of the European Union and is centrally located at the crossroads between Europe, North Africa, and the Middle

East. Given its membership in the European Union, new products created in the country can often be transposed directly into continental Europe. A security or fund that has the blessing of the Maltese regulator should carry the same stamp of approval as that of one issued by any other nation within the 28-member partnership.

Maltese laws pertaining to the digital finance space were designed to recognize the need for a complete ecosystem around security tokens. This includes outlets for trading, security promotion, infrastructure development, and investor education.

The backbone of Malta's regulatory architecture comes from legislation their parliament passed called the "Virtual Financial Assets Framework." These laws give legal footing to the security tokens and digital assets issued in the country.[4] Because of this clear direction set in place by the government, businesses know that doing projects in Malta will be legally acceptable and that regulatory guidelines will be in place so that investors and other stakeholders can more easily get comfortable with the digital space. This in turn promotes an environment that supports innovation and technological growth while simultaneously creating financial integrity and investor protections.

Bermuda   A territorial dependency of Great Britain, Bermuda has also tried to make a mark in the world of digital assets. Today, custody remains a big issue that prevents the rapid adoption of digital currencies for institutional investors. Bermuda has decided to adopt laws that are inviting and attracting custodians and is granting these critical service providers a place in which to experiment with holding digital assets and show the world their custodial capabilities. Also, in 2018, regulators within the Bermuda Business Development Agency passed legislation called the Digital Asset Business Act to create a framework for hosting Fintech companies involved in blockchain.[5]

Gibraltar   Gibraltar is also an overseas territory of the United Kingdom. Located at the southern tip of Spain on a body of water that separates Europe from Africa, Gibraltar's economy is based on services such as banking, online gambling, and insurance – and most of its clients are based outside its borders. In early 2018, Gibraltar issued the Distributed Ledger Technology Regulatory Framework, a piece of legislation designed to attract companies in the blockchain industry. The country has given licenses to five crypto exchanges and the country's trade minister has made a commitment to create a "supportive environment" for the sector.

The Gibraltar Stock Exchange has made clear to the world its intention to be a cutting-edge player in the security token markets. By working with regulators and investing in technologies, the Gibraltar Stock Exchange is looking to further develop its capabilities to trade and maintain a security token presence.[6]

Bahamas   The Commonwealth of the Bahamas has announced its intention to be a leading hub for blockchain. The country sees the new technology as having the potential to transform its economy and modernize its financial infrastructure. The nation's parliament has enacted the Digital Assets and Registered Exchange Bill, or DARE Bill, to promote the formation, promotion, maintenance, sale, and redemption of initial token offerings in the Bahamas. This legislation aims to promote the country as a premier jurisdiction for blockchain start-ups and companies looking to utilize the technology. The country has also created a framework around digital identity as well as around the acceptance of cryptocurrencies as payment in kind for securities.[7]

The Bahamas already boasts a strong financial sector with over 250 licensed banks and trust companies. On top of that, the nation has long been seen as a tax friendly environment – this includes a 20-year exemption for foreign corporations and their shareholders. The combination of these initiatives is likely to make the Bahamas a jurisdiction for the financial industry to keep its eye on.

> "Digitization of our government and financial services complements both our ease of doing business initiatives and our digital Bahamas framework. As a first step in our ease of doing business initiative, we would have moved to a new online interface for start-up companies registering their business for the first time in The Bahamas."
>
> K. Peter Turnquest, Deputy Prime Minister and Minister of Finance of the Bahamas[8]

Key Countries

While it is more likely that the groundbreaking work and legislation will first be passed in smaller countries, the world's largest economies will have to take part in order for tokenization to be a successful trend. The majority of the world's wealth is located in just a few countries – without their inclusion, security tokens will remain a side note. In fact, the world's three richest countries, the US, China, and Japan, have a total wealth just shy of $175 trillion; this is more than the next 150 countries combined! (Figure 7.1)

United States   Given its high standing in both the world of finance and technology, the United States is a country with the resources and expertise to drive the development and adoption of security tokens and other digital assets. Many companies and business leaders in the United States have been quite vocal about the potential that blockchain holds for the financial industry and society. Hundreds of millions of dollars and countless hours have been invested in the United States toward taking blockchain to the next level.

Currently the biggest inhibitors that entrepreneurs, companies, and investors are faced with in the United States are the country's stringent and unclear regulatory policies. The Securities and Exchange Commission, or SEC, is a key governing body that needs to signoff on rules that pertain to the tokenization of assets. The SEC has made it clear that security tokens will be regulated just like any other security.

FIGURE 7.1   Aggregated Wealth by Country

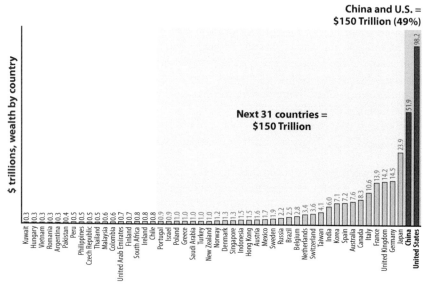

Source: Credit Suisse Research Institution[9]

> "A note for professionals in these markets: those who engage in semantic gymnastics or elaborate structuring exercises in an effort to avoid having a coin be a security are squarely within the crosshairs of our enforcement division."
>
> Jay Clayton, Chairman of the SEC, on digital assets[10]

The key piece of regulatory framework that legislators will look to in the United States to determine if indeed a digital asset should be deemed a security is known as the Howey Test. The **Howey Test** is a precedent set by the United States Supreme Court and is used to determine if investments are deemed securities. Per the Howey Test, these four criteria must be met for an asset to be classified as a security:[11]

- An investment of money is made.
- There is an expectation of profit.
- A common enterprise is present.
- A third party or promoter generates the profit.

As security tokens represent the ownership of rights and economic incomes from the assets behind them, they can indeed be regarded as securities in the eyes of the regulators and thus are held to a greater level of legal scrutiny. The exact regulations imposed will be dependent on the characteristics of the underlying asset.

Warning shots have been fired at those who try to abuse the security token industry and that egregious examples of fraud will be handled accordingly. On top of all this, there are many other regulatory entities in the United States that will also need to get on board so that large financial institutions and retail investors will become more comfortable investing in security tokens, including the Commodity Futures Trading Commission, the US Department of Treasury, and others.

Progress has been made in the United States toward developing a regulatory environment that enables an investor-friendly market for security tokens with appropriate safeguards. Time and testing will be needed as further steps are taken, but it seems clear that regulators in the United States are keen to stay at the cutting edge of digitization.

Case Study: Ripple

In 2012, Ripple Labs of California released the Ripple payment protocol to provide "secure, instantly and nearly free global financial transactions of any size with no chargebacks." Core to the Ripple payments protocol were two components: the XRP ledger and the XRP token.

Built with distributed ledger technology, the XRP ledger was developed as a peer-to-peer network to serve as a universal payments system to facilitate the transfer of funds across international borders. Ripple Labs saw the need for financial institutions to simplify cross-border payments infrastructure. Prior to the launch of the Ripple protocol, banks traditionally used the SWIFT banking network to enable international payment orders – albeit at a much higher cost. XRP tokens are used to represent the transfer of value across the Ripple network. The cumulative value of all XRP tokens is so high that it consistently ranks in the Top 3 of all cryptocurrency projects. [12,13]

What makes the XRP ledger so attractive is that transaction fees are negligible and settlement times are as little as a few seconds – a marked improvement from the traditional 3 to 5 days it used to take for a similar operation. The system also has a processing throughput that is more than 100 times greater than that of Bitcoin or Ethereum. Customers see value, too – Ripple Labs has been able to sign up an impressive list of heavy-hitter corporations from around the world to use its services. These institutions include American Express, UBS, MoneyGram, PNC, Westpac, Santander, and Siam Commercial Bank. [14]

With all of these unique features and the clear need for this type of service, investors jumped at the idea of putting money behind the project. Money poured into the XRP tokens as the expectation of future demand was high.

One of the biggest unknowns facing Ripple Labs though is whether or not the XRP token can be considered a security. This question has been brought up on

(continued)

(continued)

numerous occasions but has never been completely settled by the SEC.[15] While British authorities, such as the Financial Conduct Authority, have expressly stated that XRP is not a security, it is the American regulators who will likely have the final say.[16] To complicate matters further, Ripple Labs faced a class action lawsuit claiming the allegation that it held an unregistered security sale of its XRP tokens. The plaintiff asserted that Ripple Labs had mislead investors and sold XRP through methods that violated US Federal security laws. This class action lawsuit has gone back-and-forth for quite some time now between both parties in the courts.

While Ripple Labs, the XRP ledger, and the XRP token are indeed separate from one another, they do still maintain an inherent interconnectivity because of the network's design. Each of the three are dependent on one another while benefiting and complementing one another. For several years, XRP utilized the Ripple logo and was commonly referred to as "Ripple"; XRP is a name that is still yet to fully catch on in the crypto community. A large supply of the XRP tokens are still held by Ripple Labs itself. The company sells XRP tokens into the market and discloses the amounts on a regular basis. Because of this, plaintiffs are claiming that Ripple Labs has influence on the market and price of the XRP tokens.

According to the website "XRP Ledger":

> "In 2012, the creators of the XRP Ledger (Chris Larsen, Jed McCaleb, and Arthur Britto) gave 80 billion XRP to Ripple (the company, called Open-Coin Inc. at the time) in exchange for Ripple developing and promoting the XRP Ledger. Since then, the company has regularly sold XRP, used it to strengthen XRP markets and improve network liquidity, and incentivized development of the greater ecosystem. In 2017, the company placed 55 billion XRP in escrow to ensure that the amount entering the general supply grows predictably for the foreseeable future. Ripple's XRP Market Performance site reports how much XRP the company has available and locked in escrow at present."[17]

Whether or not XRP tokens are indeed a security because of the way they are promoted by Ripple Labs is ultimately a matter for regulators and the courts. Ripple shows that there are clearly issues being debated as to whether some cryptocurrencies should be classified as securities.[18] Until these questions are answered, additional risks are a reality and adoption will be less than it would otherwise.

European Union More and more countries within the European Union are taking a pro-blockchain stance and seeking to harness the benefits of security tokens. This movement is not limited to just one or two places in Europe, rather it is quite widespread. Luxembourg issued the "National Blockchain Act" and Estonia has granted over 900 licenses to blockchain tech firms operating in their country.[19,20] Countries like France and Germany are also delving into the security token space. Recently, the German financial regulator BaFin gave clearance to the peer-to-peer lending platform, BitBond, to issue the BB1 token. This was the first instance of a major European regulator giving the go-ahead to a security token offering.[21]

The European Union Prospectus Regulation will soon go into effect and cause significant impacts on the security token space. This new set of laws should clearly outline the proper disclosures for issuing and trading of security tokens in Europe. These rules are also expected to simplify the ways in which the sponsors of projects need to disclose what they are offering.[22]

One of the biggest opportunities in security tokenization may come from smaller companies based in Europe. This is because regulations for entities that are raising less than a few million euros will not need to have their prospectus approved by a regulator and can go ahead with a direct issue of shares to the general public.[23] As a result, it is likely that many entrepreneurial endeavors and self-starter programs will take advantage of this new technology to raise seed capital.

United Kingdom For several decades, the City of London has prospered immensely due to its status as one of the premier financial market centers in the world. However, by opting for a "Brexit," the United Kingdom may see an exodus of financial businesses and professionals as they move to jurisdictions that expect to remain firmly planted within the boundaries of the EU.

Neither the British nor their politicians want to see these jobs or the monies that come along with them flee. Britain has a thriving technology community and is seen as one of the leading high-tech innovators in the world. Because of this, there may be a silver lining to Brexit. Regulators and financial professionals in the country are looking for ways to create new avenues in which to conduct financial activity in the UK. Digital securities are one of those outlets.

In July 2019 the UK Financial Conduct Authority, or FCA, delivered its guidance on which tokens would fall under his jurisdiction. The regulator determined that cryptocurrencies like Ethereum and Bitcoin should not be regulated but that anti-money-laundering rules would apply. The guidelines provided a definition for security tokens and stated that they fall under the category of a "specified investment."[24]

China As China is a land of some 1.4 billion people, the country will clearly play a pivotal role in determining the future of security tokens and digital assets. Should the nation's regulators open the doors to blockchain-based securities, it would be a major step toward mainstream global adoption.

Cryptocurrencies, and Bitcoin in particular, have had a tumultuous past decade in the world's largest nation. China's strict government intervention over its economy includes the setting of stringent exchange rate guidelines for its currency and the imposition of capital controls that limit investor ability to move money in and out of the country. This has resulted in assets with decentralized structures, like cryptocurrencies, being watched over with a careful eye as they inherently could circumvent the rules China has put in place over its markets.

There have been periods when China has placed outright bans on its citizens' ability to legally exchange cryptocurrencies for fiat. While people could hold crypto, cashing in those holdings became difficult and could subject people to severe penalties; these rules clearly were meant to discourage citizens from utilizing digital assets.[25]

At the same time, these last several years have seen many glimmers of hope for a future where the Chinese people may be able to use blockchain in a way that is supported and encouraged by their government. Several rumors and reports are abounding that the People's Bank of China, the country's central bank, is contemplating the idea of creating its own federal cryptocurrency and is grappling with ways to best integrate one into Chinese society.[26] Also, China's Hangzhou internet court recently made a critical ruling deeming Bitcoin as a commodity because of its scarcity and abilities to carry and transfer value.[27] In July 2019, the state-run Bank of China, the world's fourth largest bank, posted graphics on its website to explain the history and inner workings of cryptocurrencies.[28] These events illustrate positive signs that China is at a minimum lukewarm to blockchain.

It will take time to see how China's role in the development of digital assets will unfold. The country's government will certainly be a critical swing factor in whether or not their adoption is successful. But China clearly realizes that blockchain technology is not going away and it is encouraging to see the government grasping the benefits that can be derived.

Japan Japan was one of the first countries to acknowledge cryptocurrencies at the regulatory level and today the Japanese are forging ahead into the expansion of the security token sector. The Financial Services Agency, or FSA, is one of Japan's key government agencies overseeing the financial industry and has begun to categorize the way security tokens are governed under Japanese laws. Security tokens must adhere to strict registration requirements and will be required to provide semiannual reports and maintain records around ownership.[29]

In October 2019, six major Japanese brokerage firms launched the Japan STO Association. The list of banks included SBI, Monex, Rakuten Securities, Nomura, Daiwa, and Mitsubishi UFJ. This news is extraordinary – given the fact that Mitsubishi UFJ is the world's sixth largest bank in terms of assets means that major financial institutions are truly taking a look at security tokens and are interested in their future and development. The association will be headquartered in Tokyo and the group will support the development of security token fundraising in accordance with all applicable laws and investor protections.[30]

These steps suggest that Japan remains committed to a plan to foster the development of blockchain-based securities.

Industry Trends: Central Bank Digital Currencies

In October 2019, Chinese leader Xi Jinping made a definitive statement that blockchain was "an important breakthrough" and that China needed to "seize the opportunity." In making this proclamation, Xi lauded the country's plans to foster the research, development, and standardization of blockchain technologies. Xi emphasized that taking these steps toward digitalization would bring about profound economic and social benefit. In making these announcements, Xi became the first major world leader to publicly endorse the merits of blockchain and distributed ledger technology. By doing so, he put the initiative's development in a place of high stature.

This declaration created quite a bit of buzz within China and brought about a slew of new projects. China became committed to increased education, investment, and innovation in the blockchain realm. Corporations in China shortly thereafter announced a number of goals and proposals to take the country forward.[31]

One of the most talked about ambitions though was the People's Bank of China's efforts to launch a digital currency electronic payments system – one which could potentially replace cash with a blockchain-based solution. This project has the potential to make China the first major economy in the world to employ a native digital currency. The digital Yuan would be a powerful monetary force which China could use as she expands influence and investment overseas.

Other nations are following suit. Around the world, country leaders are talking up their ambitions to create national stablecoins while others are actually taking action. For example, the Central Bank of the Bahamas is planning to issue its own digital currency through an initiative called "Project Sand Dollar." In light of the damage that occurred due to Hurricane Dorian, the Bahamas wants to ensure its economic resilience in light of another natural disaster and is looking to release its new digital currency sometime in 2020. By having a digital currency, the Bahamas will partially free itself from cash and the need to quickly reopen banks in the case of another disaster.[32]

Second, the Republic of the Marshall Islands has set forth plans to create its own national digital currency as a way to lessen the country's dependence on the US dollar. The new currency will be called the Marshallese Sovereign and is expected to contain built-in compliance features as well as a mechanism to grow the supply of the currency at a rate of 4% per year. By using transparent blockchain technology, the Marshall Islands hopes to develop its own predictable, reliable currency to act as a store of value and viable means of exchange.[33]

Chapter Summary

Regulation is a complex and tedious topic; abiding by the appropriate rules and regulations is the first and most critical step when issuing a security token. The actual rules for security tokens will be determined at the local jurisdictional level and legislation is not yet fully developed. This section was meant to give high-level summaries of what is happening with security tokens from a regulatory standpoint and to review the key fundamental aspects to think about when evaluating a jurisdiction's regulatory landscape. It is always advisable to consult legal counsel before making any decisions around investments or incorporation.

- In order to achieve broader acceptance, security tokens will need to embrace regulation and best compliance practices.
- Uncertainties around regulation are one of the biggest challenges hindering the development of security tokens for the broader public.
- Society's perception of digital securities has been marred by negative events – particularly those relating to cryptocurrencies. This doubt causes regulators to move slowly and forces entrepreneurs to develop highly secure solutions.
- Countries around the world view security tokens with a wide array of opinions. Smaller nations tend to be at the forefront of creating a digital friendly environment and regulatory framework.
- In order for security tokens to be a global phenomenon, key places such as the United States, China, Japan, and the European Union will need to eventually get on board. This is because most of the world's wealth resides in those regions.

CHAPTER 8

MARKETS FOR DIGITAL ASSETS & SECURITY TOKENS

- Tokens are inherently more tradable and offer more functionality than paper certificates.
- Tokenization will improve options for liquidity and reduce frictions around trading.
- Security tokens offer the potential to reduce or even eliminate settlement and clearing costs, times, and risks.

Trading & Finding Liquidity

In the future, stocks, bonds, commodities, and other financial instruments and assets will be tokenized. Security tokens are inherently easier to trade because they offer more features and have fewer frictions than do their paper alternatives. What will truly make the move to digitalization so pivotal is that one day you could have a global decentralized market for liquidity for all of these assets. As more assets become tokenized, cross-border trading will be less difficult and transfer of ownership will become nearly instantaneous. Investors will have the ability to trade 365 days a year, 24 hours a day. Smart contracts and protocols should create an environment of limited counterparty risks and faster transfer of ownership.

Before going further, a little more clarity about "liquidity" should be provided. Liquidity is a market feature that allows participants to buy or sell something quickly, without the order causing a meaningful change in the asset's price. Liquidity is related to the amount of trades that occur in a market (commonly referred to as trading volume) and can also be measured by observing the price impacts from such trades. Typically, this is done by calculating bid–ask spreads at various points over a given period. A market will generally be considered "liquid" if there is little to no waiting time in finding a suitable counterparty with whom to trade at mutually acceptable terms. "Illiquid," however, does not necessarily mean that one is "unable to trade" – it could simply imply that an asset is costly to trade or that it is slow to move at a desired price or over a given time frame. This could be because it is difficult to match up with an appropriate counterparty or because significant paperwork and other hurdles have to be addressed. Security tokens and an electronic marketplace can provide remedies to alleviate these situations.

Public securities generally have market depth and high liquidity especially when compared to private securities. Minority stakeholders in public securities have the right to move in and out of positions as they desire. But there is a big cost in taking an asset public in today's traditional market. There are significant fees incurred in conducting an initial public offering as well as in complying with the ongoing processes that regulatory bodies require from a reporting and maintenance standpoint. Because of these burdens, it is often not economical to go public unless the offering is of such magnitude that it generates the scale needed to offset the increased expenditures.

This is why tokenization creates an incredible opportunity for many projects. Costs for creating the digital wrapper are falling and the time it takes to place an asset on the blockchain so that it may traded is becoming shorter.

Gaining this liquidity will be a key driver in moving forward the trend toward digitization. Simply putting an asset on the blockchain does not in and of itself create additional liquidity. But what it certainly does do is create the optionality of liquidity and the likelihood that transactions will occur with reduced frictions. This attribute adds a dimension of sophistication to any asset and likely increases its value to investors.

But there is a Catch-22 in creating liquidity for security tokens: Why go through the cost of issuing a digital security if there are currently no secondary markets on which to trade them? Then again, why would we develop a secondary market for security tokens if there are not yet an abundance of issued tokens to trade? This dilemma of circumstances makes it hard to get a fully operating market up and running. How we get to a point of critical mass is the focus of this chapter.

Developing the Primary Markets

Security tokens have the potential to challenge the traditional initial public offering (or IPO) method for raising capital. With enhanced capabilities and the potential for lowering funding costs, digitization offers a superior path for the future. By facilitating smaller issue sizes, smaller investment tickets, and higher-caliber functionality, blockchain will provide accessibility to trillions of dollars' worth of assets to the capital markets.

The exact manner by which a new security token will be taken to market will be highly dependent on the regulations of the jurisdiction where it will be issued.

The governing body will have its own list of requirements and procedures that will have to be met prior to a successful issue. As those rules greatly vary and are subject to change, this chapter will have to confine its analysis to some major terms and issues that are likely to be faced regardless of country or region.

Accredited Investors – In an effort to protect the public, most major jurisdictions will only allow certain investments to first be distributed to persons or entities that have a sophisticated knowledge of investing. Although regulators will want to promote entrepreneurial activities and certain types of ventures, they will also want to protect persons who cannot afford to sustain heavy losses if prospects falter. As a result, regulators typically try to take a more balanced approach by providing rules that pertain to accredited investors.

Accredited investors are generally required to possess certain attributes that regulators deem appropriate. Examples of characteristics needed to gain certification as an accredited investor might include earning above a specified level of income, or having a net worth exceeding a certain threshold, or holding specific licenses. This generally includes wealthy individuals, financial institutions, large corporations, and investment vehicles such as venture-capital firms, hedge funds, and private equity firms. The specific qualifying criteria will be set by agencies like the SEC and are designed to make sure that the right type of candidate is suited for an investment.

Promoters selling securities are required to verify whether a prospective customer is an accredited investor before selling types of ventures. The process of confirming an investor's accreditation can be costly. This is why turning to third-party services such as validators can help reduce the time and risk necessary to find suitable capital.

Crowdfunding – Many projects have turned to the internet to raise money. Crowdfunding is a collaborative way to obtain funds from a large number of people and tens of billions of dollars worldwide are raised this way annually. Crowdfunding can be used for more than just investments. With this innovative model, ventures looking to sell ownership stakes or issue debt can go directly to investors to obtain capital. Crowdfunding can accelerate the process of bringing a product or service to market and can lower startup costs. Tokenization seems to be a natural fit for this type of funding.

The Jobs Act of 2012 helped pave the way for investment crowdfunding in the United States and served as a model for other countries to follow. Due to what can be an anonymous nature of crowdfunding, regulators have tried to take steps to prevent fraudulent activities and the passing of money between nefarious actors.

Crowdfunding will allow issuers to sell shares or debt in a project in exchange for the money pledged. Smart contracting and token issuing mechanisms can be put in place to help make sure that the projects offered actually get done as advertised and investors receive their due.

Lock-Ups – Some investments require a specified window of time to pass before they are eligible to be sold or redeemed. Lock-up periods can often be required by regulators or by the project itself. There could be several good reasons to prevent a new owner from selling. This could include maintaining market stability, preserving market liquidity, retaining management or key employees, or to instill a general sense of confidence about a project's future.

Security tokens offer the ability to embed time restrictions into the tokens themselves. This should reduce the amount of oversight needed to ensure securities are not sold before a predetermined moment – the tokens would theoretically be unable to be transferred prior to a certain point in time. This feature provides increased flexibility around an investment and should lessen the onus of regulatory burdens or project-imposed promises.

Bringing the Token to Market

There are three basic ways to bring a token to market and raise cash for a project. When gathering money for an endeavor, promoters and investors need to be first and foremost aware of what the token is intended and designed to do. Only after doing so can the issuer and their lawyers properly determine what types of regulations and investor protections are needed to ensure a successful issue that is compliant and free from legal liabilities.

The three major types of issuance are often referred to as:

ICO – Initial Coin Offering
IEO – Initial Exchange Offering
STO – Security Token Offering

The chart below provides a good high-level understanding of what each token offering is intended to do and the characteristics that pertain to each form of fundraising.

Comparison Between ICO, IEO, and STO

	ICO (Initial Coin Offering)	IEO (Inital Exchange Offering)	STO (Security Token Offering)
Definition	Crowdfunding by issuing utility token/coin	Crowdfunding by issuing utility token/coin via cryptocurrency exchange	Crowdfunding via issuing asset-backed token/coin
Difficulty to Set Up	Easy	Medium	Hard
Fundraising Cost	Low	Medium	High
Investor Protection	Low	Medium	High
Investor Accessibility	High	Medium	Low
Regulation Level	Low	Medium	High
Governance Level	Loose	Medium	Tight
Liquidity	Medium	High	Low

Source: Kodorra.com[1]

Developing Secondary Markets

Exchanges and other trading venues are an essential piece of the security token ecosystem, as they provide an outlet for liquidity and access to tokenized offerings. The financial industry is learning that it is indeed possible to have security exchanges operating on the basis of distributed ledger technology. Professional traders are getting involved and building the necessary infrastructure quickly. Trading platforms that have transparency and that operate in a regulatory friendly, safe, and secure way will soon be able to provide a place where securities will find ordinary price discovery. This is an exciting step for the digitization of securities because soon, in theory, anyone with an internet connection, sufficient resources, and the proper legal credentials will have the ability to access the capital markets.

The public markets that are being built for security tokens will be far different from what we have seen from those used for cryptocurrency trading. Markets for products like Bitcoin are not regulated and have not provided the appropriate means to unwind trades or custody securities. This has led to a constant set of revolving headlines around fraud and high-profile hackings. As we move away from this "Wild West" way of trading Bitcoin and into a more regulated setting, investors will find the stringent controls and compliance mechanisms of a world-class marketplace.

Regulators are on heightened alert to protect investors and will take actions to do so. Any firm looking to offer trading in security tokens and other digital assets will need to take note. This will undoubtedly initially cause costs to increase and require more ongoing reporting requirements. It will also force trading venues to be quite selective in which tokens they list. Offerings will need to have been issued correctly and have the best implementation of proper KYC and AML procedures so as not to pose unnecessary liability on the platform or its users.

In creating a viable digital secondary marketplace, three things are needed:

1. Exchanges and Trading Venues – This includes building a critical mass of users and offerings, implementing the proper rules and enforcement mechanisms, and obtaining appropriate regulatory sign-offs.
2. Financial Services and Value-Added Assistance – This can include myriad options, including helping projects to raise capital, offering and promoting assistance in best governance practices, the facilitation of accurate and timely disclosure of records, and empowering national or supranational legal frameworks.
3. Technology – This means having the infrastructure to automate, facilitate, and promote the end-to-end needs in making a trade. Exchanges can differentiate themselves by having the most sophisticated processes to stimulate productivity, efficiency, and advancement. Without leading-edge computer and network technologies, the necessary scale and speed to effectively operate would not be possible.

Case Study: Singapore's iSTOX Digital Platform

The Southeast Asian nation of Singapore is widely considered one of the most forward thinking and innovative capitalist bastions in the world. The country has long been lauded for its flexible regulatory environment and leading-edge technological infrastructure. This reputation has consistently made Singapore a leading financial hub in Asia. As a result, Singapore boasts a vibrant wealth management and capital markets industry.

Singapore is looking to capture a piece of the incredible potential the future holds for digital securities. SGX is a holding company that owns and operates the Singapore Exchange, the leading bourse for securities and derivatives in the country. Under the guidance of the Monetary Authority of Singapore, SGX has developed iSTOX – a new platform aiming to be a one-stop solution for the issuance, custody, and trading of digital securities. iSTOX will create a bridge that connects investors straight to issuers by providing seamless access to banking, brokerage, exchange, and clearing mechanisms.[2] This platform should make Singapore one of the leading places in the world to issue and trade security tokens (Figure 8.1).

By utilizing blockchain, iSTOX integrates the steps needed to open up investment opportunities that were once out of reach to many people. The platform

FIGURE 8.1   iSTOX Offerings

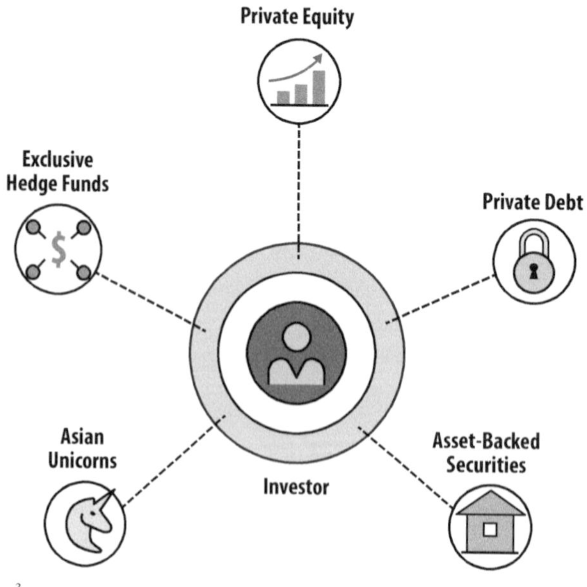

Source: iStox[3]

will create a liquidity engine for private equity, private debt, and alternative investment products. iSTOX will provide robust screening and approval processes to all investment opportunities offered on its exchange. This will ensure that only reputable and high-quality projects are available. By linking investors directly to the investments, iSTOX will cut out unnecessary fees and headaches while providing rapid settlement and trusted protection mechanisms. DBS, the largest bank in the region, will provide custody of tokens and client funds. These services will create an end-to-end, user-friendly customer experience.

Trading houses from around Asia have put substantial capital into this project. Tokai Tokyo of Japan, Hanwha Asset Management of Korea, and Phatra of Thailand are all shareholders. Temasek, the sovereign wealth fund of Singapore, is a major investor as well. iSTOX has also developed key partnerships with many highly respected companies such as PwC, Deloitte, and leading Asian law firms. SGX has recruited many key employees to fill critical positions for compliance and security.

In February 2020, the Monetary Authority of Singapore greenlit iSTOX's operations and provided a full license for its capital markets business. This announcement made iSTOX the world's first regulated and licensed digital securities platform.[4]

> "We see iSTOX as a potential disruptor in the traditional capital markets. Via digitised security issuance on iSTOX, companies and asset owners have another option to raise capital. For investors, they now have a broader investment opportunity set."
> Derek Lau, CEO of Heliconia Capital – an investment unit of Temasek[2]

> "We believe iSTOX will be the future of capital markets. With cutting-edge technological capabilities, this platform will make fundraising near-frictionless for issuers and uncover a vast array of investment opportunities for investors. Also, being based in Singapore, iSTOX will benefit greatly from its forward-looking regulatory regime and robust financial ecosystem."
> Aphinant Klewpatinond, CEO of Kiatnakin Phatra Financial Group[2]

What Is Needed for Tokenization to Thrive?

The market will have to evolve toward a decentralized token exchange. Centralized exchanges though are often more user-friendly, more likely to obtain regulatory approval, and are built to access traditional capital. But in taking this route that seems easier in the short term, you end up back where you started in some ways.

You are stuck with an intermediary all over again! In many ways, the whole point of the blockchain is that everyone using the system is working off the same ledger to enforce mutually beneficial guidelines. If we revert back to one centralized location, then what is the point of using blockchain?

In the world of finance though, there are rarely perfect solutions and if we can get to a point where a centralized exchange or competing centralized exchanges are utilizing blockchain as a way to facilitate transactions, we will have made major progress and will be on a better path than what we are on today.

If we can get to a stage where we use a decentralized exchange, the barriers to listing and trading tokens will be much smaller. But this will force individual investors to rely more on smart contracts and to do more research on the investment fundamentals of the tokens themselves.

Security token standards and protocols also need to be further developed, accepted, and implemented throughout the industry so that such tokens can be transferred freely across decentralized platforms. Only then will the integration mechanics needed for exchanges to enable anyone to trade be present. A properly functioning market cannot be continuously crafting bespoke solutions for each new offering. Uniform criteria across all security tokens will allow trading to occur regardless of how the issuer created its digital securities. These top-to-bottom levels of sophistication will produce a new type of globalized market that will simplify trading and help get us to a point where price discovery and liquidity can be met.

Jurisdictions

When finding the appropriate licenses and regulatory approvals to open a trading platform, everything starts with jurisdiction. The way governments function around the world varies greatly as do the priorities of the leaders running them.

Some countries are making it a priority to foster innovation in financial services and technology. Security tokens and the subsequent ecosystem being built around them can provide a good alternative for cutting-edge leaders to latch onto.

Trailblazers in the blockchain community have been actively taking the lead in working with regulators in these countries. And in some smaller countries, it may be easier and more convenient for the regulators and those employed in the security token industry to work together. Security token participants and pioneers may be more likely to have a greater voice with regulators in these markets. And by having the regulator's ear, one is more likely to foster mutual cooperation. Regulators and members of the financial community will likely begin to compromise with one another so as to create a solution that is beneficial to the country as a whole.

In places where the government wants to grow its jurisdiction's standing by holding itself out as "digital friendly," you'll be more likely to see groundbreaking developments and experimentation. Other nations will look to these countries who are at the forefront for guidance.

Alternative Trading Systems

Over twenty years ago, the Securities and Exchange Commission, or SEC, introduced Regulation ATS to provide alternative means for investors to access liquidity. This rule permitted the creation of alternative trading systems. **Alternative trading systems**, commonly referred to as ATSs, are venues that typically register as broker-dealers and match the buy and sell orders of its subscribers. Unlike an exchange, an ATS does not set specific rules for its users, other than standard codes of conduct. These trading platforms are not registered as exchanges themselves but can deal in securities listed on national exchanges.[5]

In June 2018, the SEC amended some of its rules around ATSs that should help foster their use in the trading of security tokens. The SEC's actions intensified public disclosure requirements for ATSs, improved operational transparency of these venues, and limited potential conflicts of interest. The additional clarity around regulated ATSs should facilitate the creation of secondary market trading of security tokens.[6] Token trading is now occurring on these venues and this trend will be closely watched by institutions and other investors who are looking to get involved in digital assets.

The debut of trading on ATSs may also be looked back upon as a watershed event in the market for start-up companies. Investments in early stage firms often have limited opportunity to find liquidity. As a result, it can often be several years before someone can realize a cash return on investment. While lock-up periods may still be in force, ATS platforms should be able to provide an outlet for people looking to sell their positions in venture opportunities.

Special Considerations Around Private Assets

Security tokens have the potential to cause major disruption in the world of private assets. By offering a digitized form of ownership, projects will reduce the time, resources, and connections needed to raise capital. This is because asset digitalization is creating a whole new user experience, new possibilities that were previously unavailable. Digitizing an asset and using a smart contract enables owners to liquidate their holdings of private securities on complaint exchanges on-demand. This new way of representing ownership will provide tremendous benefits to both promoters and the end consumer.

Larger, More Diverse Investor Bases – The ability to fractionalize ownership and subsequently sell those shares on a regulated secondary market provides an incredible opportunity for privately held assets. Investors with a large portion of a particular project can sell off their stake if desired in a piecemeal fashion overtime. This should cause less disruption in the asset's price than if one or just a few buyers is mandatory. By selling to a greater number of investors, this could also lead to a more stable and diverse shareholder base. Formerly, these private investments were just accessible to those investors with large capital and the ability to take on longer holding horizons.

Illiquidity Discounts – With today's private assets, there are many opportunities that force investors to be locked up for many years. Often these investments have no redemption features and the owners must wait until the time comes when the assets are liquidated and capital can be returned. These types of prospects are often inappropriate for some investors because they may find a need for cash before the time of liquidation comes. As a result, many will shy away from these sorts of productive opportunities.

The investment promoter should not be worried if the ownership claims can be transferred in the secondary market. So long as there are no needs for redemptions of the underlying asset or fund itself, the project will not face unwanted constraints. With security tokens, owners will have more flexibility to meet their cash flow needs and this additional liquidity should help to unlock the discounted price of the opportunity.

The difference in value between a public asset and an identical private one is often referred to as the "illiquidity discount," or sometimes as the "liquidity premium" – this difference often ranges between 20% and 30% of the public asset's value.[7] Ouch! This represents a huge amount of value and therein creates a tremendous opportunity from utilizing security tokens. Security tokens offer an option for these projects to find an easier outlet for liquidity. Through the use of ATSs, bulletin boards, and exchanges, matching buyers and sellers will come more naturally.

Transfer Fees – Tokenizing relatively illiquid assets by digitizing title and creating a market for trading can substantially reduce the frictions around changes in ownership. Today, depending on the asset itself and other factors, transfer fees can range anywhere from 2% to 15%.[8] Payments to lawyers, brokers, notaries, accountants, and other service providers can really add up with these deals. On top of this, it can take incredibly long amounts of time before title can clear. Blockchain wrappers should reduce these fees below 1% and eliminate transfer times, so this aspect is truly revolutionary and disruptive.[9]

Settlement and Clearing

Distributed ledger technologies that serve as the backbone of security tokens will assist in creating a modern clearing and settlement platform. In finance, assets can be traded on an exchange or over the counter. When a trade is executed, two parties agree to swap one asset for another. Typically, cash is involved on at least one side of the trade. This agreement is merely a promise that is dictated by the rules of the exchange or the agreed-upon terms of the parties involved. The actual transfer of assets will then take place after a set of standard processes and checks are conducted. **Clearing** is the process that turns the promise of payments into the actual movement of money from one party to another. **Settlement** is the process whereby securities are delivered to fulfill promised obligations. In the case of securities trading, it takes at least one or more business days to post a trade's execution before the actual assets change hands legally.

It may be easier if we think about the processes of clearing and settlement in terms of something else familiar. In the United States, when a home is sold on the market, a buyer contracts with the seller to purchase the house at an agreed-upon price, on an agreed-upon date, subject to agreed-upon terms. But this is not the final step in the deal. There is a time lag known as the "closing period" that happens before the actual ownership is transferred. During this window, various processes are undertaken to ensure the agreeing parties are getting exactly what they bargained for. The title to the home is checked for any deficiencies, validation of the buyer's ability to obtain credit is taken, and the house is inspected to uncover any problems that parties may not have been privy to at the time of the agreed-upon sale. These, and others, are some of the steps commonly taken to ensure a clean sale. The process of closing in the real estate market is conceptually similar in many ways to the clearing and settlement processes in the securities markets. This type of thinking can provide a framework on how to contemplate the fundamentals of clearing and settlement.

Settlement Risk

Settlement risk is the threat that one of the counterparties in a transaction fails to successfully deliver on his or her end of the trade agreement. This term can also cover the unintended consequences that can happen, for whatever reason, should the settlement processes not be completed acceptably on time. Reasons could include political changes, natural disasters (including global pandemics and shutdowns!), systemic shocks, and other perils that prevent or delay settlement from happening. While settlement risk is rare, the occurrence and perception of an occurrence is heightened during times of financial strain. In the event the settlement processes fail, it is possible that one or more counterparties are left with substantial losses.

The digitization of securities creates a situation where trades and settlement can occur simultaneously. In the past, it could take a minimum of three business days post–trade transaction before securities and cash were actually exchanged. If there were holidays and weekends involved, it would take longer. Security tokenization allows for the merging of all layers of clearing and settlement; instead of multiple reconciliations taking place over several days, in the future, investors should be able to look forward to one instantaneous transaction.

Because of their inherent features, security tokens provide evidence of ownership that is much better than the current system. With blockchain, the chains of ownership and custody are extremely clear. The technology prevents any double accounting issues and provides more certainty as to whether the underlying asset is actually there.

Convenience and the ability to reduce risk are two of the driving reasons people will eventually gravitate toward digital securities. If people behaved perfectly in an honest and open market, settlement risk would not be a factor. We live in an imperfect world, however, and problems around settlement do occur. The trust elements of blockchain, though, have the ability to greatly reduce, or even eliminate, settlement risk. Also, the speed of completing and ease of finalizing a trade is greatly enhanced through a token. Why would anyone want to wait several days to do something if they had the option to execute it right away? Just as Netflix's DVD through the mail business eventually was dwarfed by its streaming service, financial firms delivering outdated settlement services will soon be displaced by those who provide the emerging technology. Investment firms and issuers will likely find that offering tokens is a fantastic and necessary way to please customers and investors. These reasons should provide major incentives for the financial world to adopt security tokens and their protocols.

Industry Trends: Real-Time Blockchain Settlements

Paxos Trust, a New York–based financial services institution and creator of the digital Paxos dollar, has launched a blockchain-based settlement platform for several listed companies that trade on US exchanges. Paxos has already signed up two major investment banking houses, Credit Suisse of Switzerland and Société Générale of France; both will use Paxos' services in hopes of reducing costs and modernizing their financial infrastructure. The SEC has given Paxos a greenlight to do this as long as the initial volumes of trades it clears will be less than 1% of a stock's total traded volume. This should provide Paxos with a good reference implementation to prove if its systems are indeed capable and reliable.[10]

Historical Perspective: The Global Financial Crisis of 2008

In September 2008, pandemonium swept through the global financial markets. The crisis had started about a year earlier in subprime mortgages and in firms that had taken on too much debt. As time went on, the calamity spread into real estate, banking, and just about every other part of the economy.

As prices fell, the markets panicked. While there were many factors at play, the immediate need for cash at several large institutions exacerbated the downward spiral. The current financial system is based on the premise that the exchange of payment and securities will take place days, and sometimes even weeks, after a trade is executed in the marketplace. This significant lag in time occurs when settling virtually every type of transaction. This system inevitably caused the problems of the financial crisis to be deeper and more widespread.

Why was this the case? As was just mentioned, several large entities needed cash immediately to meet liquidity and regulatory requirements to satisfy lenders and regulators – many mortgage companies, banks, and broker-dealers were on the brink of insolvency and the counterparties to whom they were planning to sell their assets could not take the risk of receiving money days in the future. This made the financial system incredibly fragile and showed that the downfall of any one financial institution could infect the system at large. Should any counterparty go insolvent, there would be no way to resolve the outstanding and pending positions as the chain of ownership would be broken. Markets froze as a result and prices plummeted to unthinkably low levels. This crisis illustrated that our financial framework is under constant settlement risk.

In the future, settlement risk may become a thing of the past as blockchain technology eliminates the need for a transition period between trade date and settle date. There should never be any debate overhanging the transfer of title with security tokens and the essential ingredient of any successful market – trust – is never questioned. Thus, the transparency, timeliness, and efficiencies of security tokens can create a more vibrant and stable financial marketplace.

Where These Markets Are Going

It is likely that digital asset trading will soon mushroom with growth. The potential for improved contractual performance, reduced counterparty risk, instant settlements, and better structuring of financial products provides too much incentive to be overlooked. There have been many clear breakthroughs already. For example, Swiss security laws allow for settlement on the blockchain. Retail portals that are powered on mobile apps are a reality and being improved upon consistently. Jurisdictions in Europe and Africa have permitted the creation of the first fully regulated security tokens. More exciting stories, products, and possibilities turn up almost daily. Many believe that security tokens will become so popular that they will eventually replace Over-the-Counter markets and traditional stock exchanges. The boundaries around the possibilities of what can be done with security tokens are theoretically endless – we have an incredible ride ahead of us!

Industry Trends: Stock Exchanges & Distributed Ledger Technology

Around the world, established stock exchanges are embracing distributed ledger technology and blockchain as a way to prepare themselves for the oncoming changes to our financial market infrastructure. These organizations understand how this new technology will transform the future of money and how we invest as a society. Here is a look at a few examples of how world-class organizations have already taken steps towards adoption:

- The Securities and Exchange Board of India has established an advisory committee to explore ways in which blockchain can improve and deepen the Indian securities market. The country's National Stock Exchange, based in Mumbai, is testing blockchain through proof-of-concept methods to learn more about how smart contracts and other facets of the technology can improve the efficiencies and transparency of its financial systems.[11,12]
- Deutsche Börse is the largest stock exchange group in Germany and together with telecom giant Swisscom is building "a trusted digital asset ecosystem." Their ambition is to create a new set of processes that can handle the issuance, custody, and trading of securities using blockchain technology. Deutsche Börse has also

announced its intention to develop a blockchain-based system for securities lending as well as a platform to more efficiently settle securities.[13]

- Euronext is the world's sixth largest stock exchange company and owns the Paris, Amsterdam, and Brussels stock exchanges. Euronext has invested over €5 million into Tokeny, a Fintech company that serves as a platform issuer of security tokens.[14]
- Formerly known as SWX, SIX Swiss Exchange is Switzerland's largest stock exchange and also trades other securities such as Swiss government bonds and derivative products like stock options. The company has announced its intentions to launch the new SDX trading platform, which utilizes blockchain technology to enhance trading and to enable its capabilities to handle Security Token Offerings.[15]
- The Australian Stock Exchange, or ASX, is partnering up with several Fintech companies to move its current exchange platform over to distributed ledger technology. The company hopes to have this platform up and running by the Spring of 2021.[16]
- In the third quarter of 2019, the Intercontinental Exchange launched Bakkt, a regulated infrastructure technology for digital markets. This platform enabled institutions to trade and custody crypto assets, primarily Bitcoin.

> "I have strong conviction that by driving more integration and efficiency across digital wallets, transaction processing, and payment acceptance, there are meaningful opportunities for merchants and consumers to seamlessly interact using digital assets in ways that have not been previously considered. It is often said that digital assets will be successful when consumers don't have to think about the technology underlying them."
>
> Mike Blandina, Chief Product Officer at Bakkt[17]

Chapter Summary

- Tokens are inherently more tradable and offer more functionality than paper certificates.
- Tokenization will improve options for liquidity and reduce frictions around trading.
- When taking a new token to market, issuers will have to comply with all laws in the jurisdiction of offering.
- Token trading platforms around the world are being developed with the technology, people, standards, and necessary supporting services to facilitate transfers.
- Due to superior technology, security tokens offer the potential to reduce or even eliminate settlement and clearing costs, times, and risks.
- Some countries are holding themselves out as digital-friendly jurisdictions that promote entrepreneurship in blockchain security solutions.
- The advantages of security tokens could one day lead to the displacement of over-the-counter markets and traditional stock exchanges.

CHAPTER 9

"DeFi": eLENDING AND THE FUTURE OF GETTING A LOAN

- Blockchain will greatly improve the way loans are made and serviced.
- "DeFi" will spawn a multitude of innovative new lending products.
- An entire suite of offerings has already been developed around the lending and borrowing of crypto assets.

This book's primary focus has been on securities and how blockchain will improve public financial markets. But digitization is having a profound impact on the individual and commercial lending markets as well. New products using distributed ledger technology will be developed for home mortgages, auto loans, equipment financing, and more. These avenues are another important way for society to derive significant benefits from blockchain.

As a result, "DeFi" is one of the hottest topics in the digital newsplace today. This abbreviation is short for Decentralized Finance – the space has been expanding rapidly over the last two years and is becoming more and more significant by the day. Every week, more and more projects are coming to market that utilize a decentralized approach.

As we move into the future, the lending industry will continue to see significant transformation as blockchain technology provides the potential for enormous cost savings and value-added services in the marketplace. By delivering a trusted environment for borrowers, lenders, and regulators, distributed ledger technology is reengineering the way data is shared and how lending decisions are made. These breakthroughs enable quicker and more transparent lending processing and will elevate the overall customer experience of obtaining a loan. Simultaneously, blockchain will provide a multitude of ways to protect participants' privacy, maintain up-to-date statuses, and ensure superior record keeping.

Crypto Lending & Borrowing

An entire market for borrowing and lending has been created around cryptocurrency. Today, several leading firms offer cash loans that can be collateralized with crypto or digital assets.

The concept is rather simple. A digital asset holder who wishes to obtain a loan will deposit his or her tokens with a lender. The lender will determine how much capital the borrower can receive based on several factors, including:

- The loan-to-value ratio of the desired borrowing amount in relation to the assets pledged
- The price volatility of the underlying digital collateral
- Additional risk modeling factors
- Results of standard KYC & AML checks

If all goes well with the application process, the lender will then deliver a corresponding amount of cash to the borrower based on a set of terms. Typically, these loans are over-collateralized, meaning the collateral is worth more than the amount borrowed. This means that crypto loans are likely to be less risky and have negligible chance of default as compared to conventional forms of financing. If the borrower fails to pay back what is owed, the lender should have more than enough in escrow to cover the shortfall. The lender can simply sell the digital asset in the market to obtain the funds to recover the remaining loan principal and interest due.

Once the loan is issued, the borrower will have the obligation to repay the note with interest that accrues over time. Smart contracts will monitor the value of the loan and the collateral on an ongoing basis to ensure everything is within contractual agreements. As long as the value of the collateral does not fall below a certain amount relative to the aggregate loan balance, there should not be any issues regarding collateral or margin calls. If the collateral falls too much in value relative to the loan amount, the cryptocurrency or other digital asset is sold immediately to raise the funds needed to put the loan back in good standing.

As the market for cryptocurrencies is extremely liquid (both Bitcoin and Ethereum typically see volumes in the tens of billions of dollars daily[1]), these assets are ideal to pledge against a loan. Lenders can easily sell these tokens in the marketplace at little to no cost should the borrower fail to meet the terms of agreement. Should the borrower repay the loan interest and principal in a manner acceptable with the loan agreement, the digital asset placed as collateral will be returned. (See Figure 9.1.)

FIGURE 9.1   Sample of a Digital Lending Framework

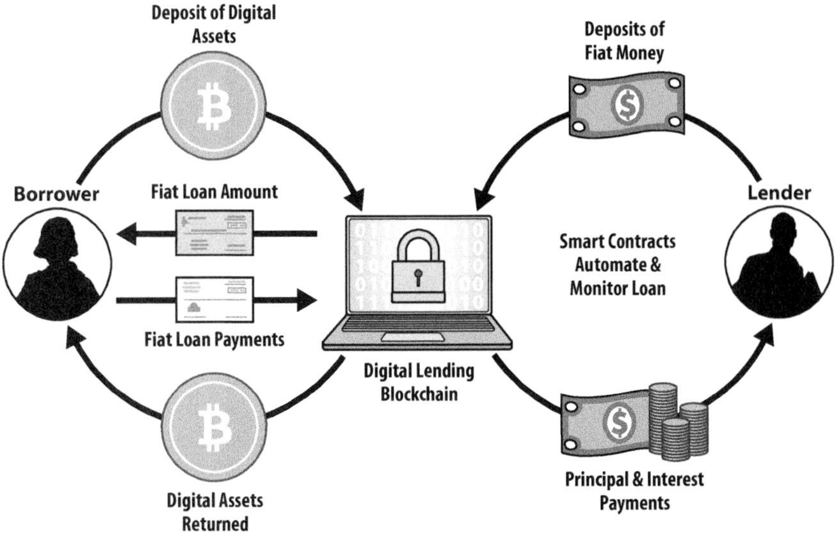

Because digital assets serve as excellent collateral, the lender has outstanding recourse if the borrower fails to make proper payments on the loan. As a result, there is minimal need for extensive credit checks on the character and capacity of the borrower. This means there is limited underwriting cost on these loans and minimal collection expenses when compared to traditional loans.

A crypto-backed loan has many appealing features to someone who is flush with digital assets. This option may be a cost-effective and efficient way to access fiat money while simultaneously maintaining control of the underlying asset. With these types of loans, users may be trying to buy homes, diversify their investment portfolios, start a new business, or pay off higher interest rate debts. By taking out a crypto-based loan, the user may be able to avoid paying taxes that could be associated with an outright sale of their cryptocurrency. Also, by taking this route, the user still participates in the upside capital appreciation the cryptocurrency may experience during the loan tenure. This permits borrowers to maintain ownership of their underlying assets while gaining access to the money they may need to fund living expenses or projects they wish to undertake.

Crypto-based lending can take several forms: loans can be made through a central custodian, through derivative type contracts, or through peer-to-peer networks. Jurisdiction is a critical factor in terms of the level of regulation to which a given lending platform will be subject and what its offerings may look like. Also, the interest rates, terms of financing, and levels of disclosure can vary widely between these platforms, so it is critical that one review the ground rules before entering an agreement.

Earn Interest on Crypto

One form of funding for these loans comes when lenders pledge cryptocurrencies to earn money. As a result, Bitcoin, Ethereum, USDCoin, or other forms of digital assets can earn interest.[2] This adds a new form of income that holders of digital assets like cryptocurrencies can earn, and provides a powerful financial tool for investors to build long-term wealth. With low or even negative interest rates in most major developed countries today,[3] this passive form of income offers an attractive relative yield.

Suppose you hold five Bitcoins and there are lending platforms that offer 5% interest on that cryptocurrency. Should you decide to deposit your tokens with the platform, you could expect to have 5.25 Bitcoins at the end of one year (your original 5 Bitcoins plus the .25 Bitcoins of interest). Your total return would include the interest you earn but also would be dependent on the fluctuation in the price of Bitcoin. While the 5% interest will certainly move your total return higher, it could easily be offset by an unfavorable move downward in the price of Bitcoin. So, lenders in this market will have to be comfortable taking the risk of volatility in the underlying cryptocurrency price. Once the speculative nature of these cryptocurrencies subsides, investors may become more comfortable with this type of income-producing investment.

One other note of caution: just as was the case for borrowers, people lending crypto as a funding source would be wise to shop terms and conditions. While the principal of earning interest with crypto is rather sound, it is still crucial to be aware of the counterparty risks. Even if the underlying loans may be good, should something go astray with the platform itself, lenders could find themselves holding the bag for the loss. As a result, the jurisdiction, credit quality, levels of disclosure, financial where-withal, access to insurance, reputation, trust, and other pertinent factors of the lending platform should all be carefully examined.

Making Loans with Blockchain

Crypto-based loans are just the first step in a much larger trend that will unfold over the coming years. Blockchain has the potential to transform the traditional ways in which we obtain a loan by simplifying, improving, and speeding up the entire financing value chain. By making loans digital, waiting times will shorten, transparency of the lending process will improve, servicing will be easier, and the documentation behind loans will be complete and securely stored.

Today's lending industry is dominated by paper-intensive processes and manual entries. These methods are prone to errors and incomplete inputs. The information used to make loans is slow to move, subject to potential manipulation, and can easily be lost, misused, or stolen.

Distributed ledger technology is ideal for driving reforms in this market. Its decentralized manner allows all parties who handle a loan to track assets, monitor financing agreements or covenants, manage cash flows, and better assess risks. If properly designed, these ledgers allow participants to maintain an accurate, real-time, and tailored workflow to monitor all steps in the loan's transfers of value. These features will allow underwriters, sponsors, rating agencies, servicers, regulators, and investors the chance to streamline operations and validate a loan's status and authenticity from start to finish.

As more and more people adopt blockchain to extend credit, markets will become freer and more transparent. Capital will be allocated more efficiently and risks will be reduced as better surveillance, stronger protections of investor rights, and seamless audit trails become a reality. In short, blockchain will help to facilitate nearly every aspect of the structure and maintenance of a loan and its lifecycle.

Mortgages

Mortgages are debt instruments which use real estate as collateral. Property purchasers will enter into a mortgage agreement to obtain funds when buying a home, office building, or other real estate. Mortgages are legal contracts that allow the lender to place a lien on the borrower's property until a loan is paid in full.

Anyone who has ever obtained a mortgage knows how tedious, time intensive, and expensive this process can be. At one point or another, you end up having to deal with all sorts of people: bank officers, mortgage brokers, accountants, real estate agents, and possibly government workers. This long, drawn-out procedure is full of regulatory and corporate hoops to jump through. You will have to provide all sorts of documentation: proof of identity, credit history, tax documents, and job verification are just a few.

Mortgage lending is a contract-intensive process. There are laws and lending standards that demand the documents behind a loan be protected and that a proper chain of custody is maintained throughout the process. Because legal protections are afforded by these documents, they have cash value attached to them. If these papers are lost, altered, or destroyed, their value is affected. To complicate things even further, today's mortgage market is highly fragmented and numerous financial institutions and other intermediaries are needed to issue a borrower money in a regulatory compliant manner. The moving around of paper between these entities can lead to all sorts of problems – lost title, lost payments, and a lack of a clear understanding as to who owns what.

Digital technologies have the potential to alter this current landscape. By using blockchain, the loan closing process is simple, intuitive, complete, and in digital format; all facets of the transaction are recorded and tracked in the ledger. Participants can apply secure digital signatures and tamperproof seals to the documents thereby ensuring their integrity throughout the process. Copies of all relevant documents are then saved securely on the blockchain and thus can be accessed at a later time if and when needed. By using distributed ledger technology, banks and other lending institutions can remove paper records from their loan originations and in so doing create a much more transparent, understandable, and easy-to-access closing process (Figure 9.2). According to a recent study by Accenture:

FIGURE 9.2 Steps in Creating a Blockchain Mortgage

How a Blockchain Mortgage Works

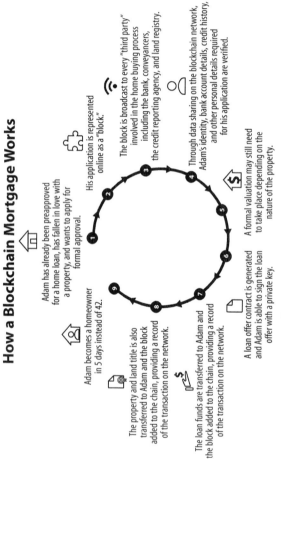

Adam has already been preapproved for a home loan, has fallen in love with a property, and wants to apply for formal approval.

His application is represented online as a "block."

The block is broadcast to every "third party" involved in the home buying process including the bank, conveyancers, the credit reporting agency, and land registry.

Through data sharing on the blockchain network, Adam's identity, bank account details, credit history, and other personal details required for his application are verified.

A formal valuation may still need to take place depending on the nature of the property.

A loan offer contract is generated and Adam is able to sign the loan offer with a private key.

The loan funds are transferred to Adam and the block added to the chain, providing a record of the transaction on the network.

The property and land title is also transferred to Adam and the block added to the chain, providing a record of the transaction on the network.

Adam becomes a homeowner in 5 days instead of 42.

Source: Home Loan Experts, homeloanexperts.com.au[5]

"The mortgage industry is a prime example of an ecosystem that would benefit from distributed ledger technology – it is a highly complex network of interwoven relationships rife with data reconciliation and validation, which add cost and time to the process. Organizing the ecosystem around a DLT platform can enable up to 80% reduction in cycle time, reducing inefficiencies and improving the customer experience. DLT can decrease loan origination costs by over 40%, with an additional 10–15% cost reduction in Servicing; overall savings for the industry is estimated at over $25 billion."[4]

Mortgages have a life cycle and go through multiple stages: the origination, property and title validation, closing, servicing, and securitization. The blockchain will ensure that all necessary steps are taken to complete a fully compliant loan. If a signature is forgotten or a mandatory data item is missing or a disclosure is not made, the blockchain will not proceed. Only after all phases are completed will the blockchain move forward. The blockchain will encrypt information and segregate data so that only the appropriate parties who are privy to specific transactions are able to read or write to the ledger. No information will be lost or fraudulently altered. These features are the prime reason why blockchain will disrupt the mortgage industry in years to come.

Case Study: Figure Technologies & the Provenance Blockchain

A home equity line of credit, or HELOC, is a loan that allows a homeowner to borrow money against the equity value of his or her house. Lenders will permit the borrower to obtain cash up to a specific amount over a predefined timeframe. Unlike a mortgage, HELOCs do not provide the borrower all funds upfront; rather, borrowers can obtain funds as needed until they reach the maximum limit of the loan agreement. A HELOC is similar to a credit card in some respects. But like a mortgage, a HELOC also uses real property as collateral. This feature typically makes the interest payments on a HELOC much lower than that of a credit card.

Because of the reduced interest rate offered by a HELOC, consumers often see this as a vehicle to consolidate their debts and reduce their monthly interest burden. The aggregate amount of home-equity in the United States is staggering; estimates for the total value are in the tens of trillions of dollars.[6] If this source of funding could be prudently utilized in a more effective and cost-efficient manner, it could improve the economy's overall health.

Unfortunately, there are many headaches to getting a HELOC. The paperwork is rather onerous and approval times can take a month or longer depending on the individual borrower's situation. The application process and resulting closing costs can get expensive quickly and ultimately make this financing option less appealing.

(continued)

(continued)

Blockchain lending start-up Figure Technologies has developed disruptive home equity lending solutions to improve the HELOC market. Through the use of its Provenance blockchain, Figure Technologies is able to originate, finance, and securitize HELOC loans. Homeowners can apply for a loan online and obtain an approval in a little as five minutes. Funding can subsequently arrive in the borrower's pocket in as little as five days later. This improvement is remarkable!

So how can Figure provide an alternative that far exceeds that of its competition? Figure uses blockchain to get rid of manual tasks and intermediaries. For example, Figure's distributed ledger technology processes eliminate the necessity of auditors, custodians, and other third parties. By cutting out these facilitators, agency costs are sliced in half.[7]

The Provenance blockchain demonstrates a proof-of-concept example of just how much mortgage-style products have to benefit from digital adoption. Provenance has already issued over $1 billion in loan originations, and company estimates calculate that over 1.25% of margin improvements have resulted due to digital efficiencies.[8] As mortgage lending is a low-single-digit margin business generally, these gains are massive. Those savings ultimately make the cost of home-ownership fall.

> "With the financing facility now in place, Provenance.io can support the entire end-to-end financing of loans, from origination to funding to servicing to financing. It paves the way for the first securitization on chain, which will demonstrate the massive cost savings, risk reduction, and liquidity benefits blockchain delivers."
>
> Mike Cagney, CEO and co-founder of Figure Technologies[9]

The future for blockchain in the lending industry is very bright. While we have only covered a few possibilities in this chapter, many other areas of lending could be tapped into as well. This could include financing for the following lines of business:

- Trade Finance & Letters of Credit
- Installment Sales
- Lease Financing
- Debt Guarantees
- Education Loans
- Agricultural Loans
- Bridge & Mezzanine Loans
- Account Receivable Financing

- Litigation Capital
- Micro Lending

There are likely many more possibilities to be explored. With the inherent transparency of the blockchain and the elimination of middlemen, lenders will earn higher returns and borrowers will enjoy lower cost of capital. All parties will experience more transparency regarding risks. The solutions brought about by blockchain have the potential to strengthen markets and increase the integrity of our financial system.

Historical Perspective: The Mortgage Crisis of 2007

From 2003 to 2006, US housing prices boomed. A strong economy, favorable demographics, legislation encouraging homeownership, and relaxed lending standards caused property values to soar. Sentiment around the real estate market was euphoric; investors were gripped by speculative fever and most believed the party would never end!

Unfortunately, the good times did not continue forever and the bubble in the US housing market burst. By 2008, the overall market was in free-fall and housing prices experienced their greatest decrease since the Great Depression.

One of the first shoes to drop happened in March 2007 when the subprime mortgage industry collapsed. Almost overnight, subprime lending companies like New Century Financial were declaring bankruptcy, suffering losses, and citing a massive uptick in delinquent loans.[10] Investors began to worry as fears mounted that the weakness of the subprime market would eventually trickle into the broader property market and economy.

Subprime lending is a type of finance that caters to people with low credit scores relative to the general public. Because of their questionable ability to repay loans, subprime borrowers pay higher interest rates and receive less favorable loan terms to compensate for their higher risk.[11]

While there are many reasons why the situation in 2007 unfolded unfavorably and why subprime lending was unsustainable, there are some facets of blockchain which, if they had been available at the time, could have helped to lessen the resulting fall. Here are a few examples of what happened in 2007 and how blockchain could prevent or alleviate this misbehavior in the future:

1. <u>Fraudulent Lending:</u> With all the easy money going around, lenders were eager to make loans and pocket commissions. Consequently, some mortgage brokers either provided inaccurate information themselves or encouraged or flat out requested borrowers to provide inaccurate information on loan

(continued)

(continued)

applications. This caused loans that would have otherwise been rejected to receive funding. With inadequate safeguards to detect bad data, investors bought loans that did not conform to the standards they were expecting. This fraud was not uncovered until the borrowers were not able to meet their payments. At that point, it was too late!

In a blockchain-based system, records can be checked against a number of sources and seamlessly entered and stored on the ledger. This information is not subject to change. This creates a transparent marketplace in which each user (or investor) can track what is really going on – and in real time.

2. Fraudulent Borrowing: Because housing prices appeared to be on a never-ending growth trajectory, many people wanted to get in on the action as fast as possible. As a result, there was no shortage of individuals who were willing to take shortcuts and undertake deceptive means when obtaining a loan. People falsified their job histories, income levels, and asset records.

Many borrowers believed that if they were to find themselves unable to pay their mortgages, their home could simply be sold quickly for a profit in the booming market. The sale proceeds would then be used to pay off the loan. Yet when the housing market came to an abrupt halt, many were left in a position where they couldn't sell their homes and prices dropped precipitously.

Had blockchain procedures been utilized during the loan origination process, red flags would have likely been detected as information about incomes and other financial factors would have been contradictory. The loans probably never would have been approved in the first place.

3. Incomplete Documentation: Regulations require a wide array of signed forms and disclosures whenever a loan is originated. If these items are not properly executed, there is an argument to be made that the loan is not legally valid.

During the mortgage crisis, many borrowers who knew they couldn't repay their loans instead took a strategy of claiming the conditions of the note were illegitimate and thus payment could not be enforced. If a borrower could show that certain signatures were missing or documents were not properly notarized or that certain facts were not divulged, then perhaps the whole loan contract should be voided to the benefit of the borrower.

At the very least, this tactic delayed investors from receiving recourse on their property and at worst resulted in investors not receiving any money back on their investments or purchased loans. Had blockchain processes been employed, all of the steps necessary for the process would have had to be followed before funds were dispersed.

4. <u>Missing Documentation:</u> During the foreclosure process, many note holders were unable to recover principal or interest because it was not possible to prove the loans were enforceable. Over time, the original documents that were used to make the loans became separated from the notes that granted title to the economic benefits of the loans themselves. Without the appropriate documentation, investors lacked proof to show they were entitled to the proceeds they expected. Paper documents in many cases were long lost or the cost of tracking them down was prohibitively expensive.[12]

Blockchain technology is inherently good at storing and maintaining high-quality records. Documents and the accompanying items needed to make them official are seamlessly stored within the blockchain itself. Thus, title to an asset is clear and easy to prove in a cost-effective manner.

Blockchain will fundamentally alter the way the financing industry operates. Companies that are early adopters of the technology will enjoy higher margins, reduced costs, fewer risks, and enhanced liquidity. Customers will appreciate the shorter approval times, reduced headaches, and lightened loads of paperwork. Ultimately, this should result in lower costs of capital and will contribute to better functioning lending markets.

Chapter Summary

- Blockchain has the potential to transform the traditional ways in which we obtain a loan by simplifying, improving, and speeding up the entire financing value chain.
- The lending industry will continue to see significant transformation as blockchain technology provides the potential for enormous cost savings and value-added services in the marketplace.
- With distributed ledger technology, banks and other lending institutions can remove paper from their loan origination processes, thereby introducing complete transparency into the closing process in an end-to-end manner.
- An entire market for borrowing and lending has been created around cryptocurrency. Today, several leading firms offer cash loans that can be collateralized with crypto or digital assets.
- Bitcoin, Ethereum, USDCoin, or other forms of digital assets can earn interest. This adds a new form of income that holders of digital assets like cryptocurrencies can earn and provides a powerful financial tool for investors to build long-term wealth.
- With the inherent transparency of the blockchain and the elimination of middlemen, lenders can earn higher returns and borrowers can enjoy lower cost of capital. Everyone is given a better opportunity to understand risks. The solutions brought about by blockchain can strengthen markets and increase the integrity of our financial system.

CHAPTER 10

DIGITAL ADOPTION

- The number of people using blockchain solutions likely will continue to rise exponentially.
- Millennials are positioned to be a key demographic for blockchain adoption.
- More work still needs to be done with blockchain-based securities around both privacy and safety.
- Events such as the COVID-19 pandemic will likely accelerate the adoption of blockchain technology and digital assets.

Where We Are Today

"Bitcoin is a classic network effect, a positive feedback loop. The more people who use Bitcoin, the more valuable Bitcoin is for everyone who uses it, and the higher the incentive for the next user to start using the technology. Bitcoin shares this network effect property with the telephone system, the web, and popular Internet services like eBay and Facebook."

Marc Andreessen, entrepreneur & investor[1]

Digital assets continue to grow in popularity throughout the world and this phenomenon has mostly been led by the expanded usage of cryptocurrency. In some ways, gravitating toward digital solutions for our money and assets is a natural extension of society's continuing reliance on the convenience of overall technology. As the internet, computers, and mobile devices achieve bigger and bigger penetration rates among the general population, it's no surprise to see people looking for ways to manage their finances directly through these linkages. As blockchain-based assets such as cryptocurrencies and security tokens continue to offer better features and functionality, the number of users should increase at a brisk rate for the foreseeable future.

Cryptocurrency Adoption

Cryptocurrency has been the typical gateway people use to first experience digital financial products. The Dutch firm ING conducts an annual study to learn more about how individuals spend, save, invest, and feel about their money. In a recent survey, the firm noted that respondents indicated that they were hearing and learning more about digital currencies. Given the dramatic uptick in the number of news articles and the rise in value of some cryptos, people are showing a keen interest in learning more about what products like Bitcoin and Ethereum are. These results tell a story that the majority of people have at least heard about the idea of cryptocurrencies – that is a pretty amazing stat on just how far digital assets have come!

One of the initial steps that has to be taken anytime a new user gets accustomed to using cryptocurrency is to first acquire a digital wallet. By measuring the growth of digital wallets, we can obtain a better understanding of how society is learning about and using cryptocurrencies. The number of wallets globally is increasing at an exponential rate and shows limited signs of leveling off.

Bitcoin Wallet Address Growth

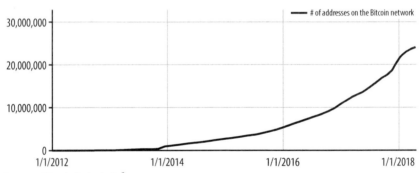

Source: Blockchain.info[3]

Demographic Synopsis

Only a small number of people own cryptocurrency and other digital assets. Studies have been commissioned to answer questions about the types of people who have taken the plunge and gotten involved. Greyscale Investments compiled a report to gain insights on how the public perceived Bitcoin as an investment vehicle. The study surveyed over 1,000 Americans in early 2019. In their conclusions, Greyscale cited that the typical investor appreciated the following aspects of Bitcoin:

- *Low minimum investment*: Respondents liked the idea of fractional ownership and that getting involved took only a small amount of initial capital. Additional purchases could be taken at a later date to scale holdings further.
- *Limited Supply*: Three quarters of participants liked that Bitcoin contained a scarcity element. The transparent methodology that Bitcoin used to keep a finite supply of coins on the market was an alluring feature.

- *Capital Appreciation Potential*: Nearly 80% of the respondents saw real potential for gains in a Bitcoin investment.

From a demographic perspective, the survey revealed some findings as to what interested investors looked like:

- *Slightly Younger Age:* Despite the stereotypical idea that cryptocurrencies are only for the youngest investors, the average age of those invested in Bitcoin was just 3 years less than the median of the general public.
- *Slightly More Conservative:* Republicans were more likely to show affinity to the Bitcoin space than Democrats.
- *More Likely to be Male:* Of the total respondents showing curiosity, 60% were men.[4,5,6]

Interest by Country

The adoption of digital assets is already a global phenomenon, yet some places have been more likely to jump aboard than others. There have been a few noticeable

FIGURE 10.1   Graphic Depicting Results from the ING International Survey on Mobile Banking

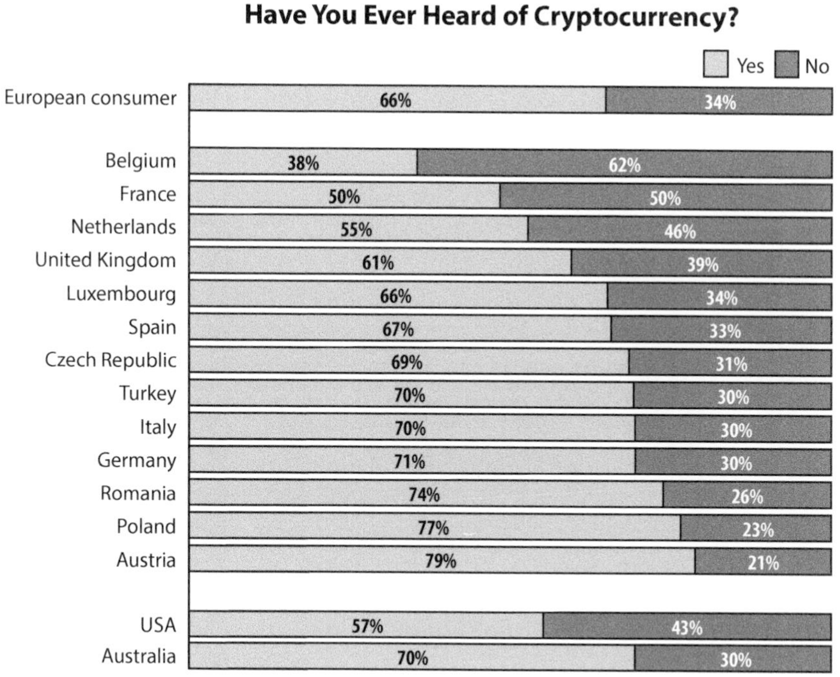

Have You Ever Heard of Cryptocurrency?

Source: ING International Survey Mobile Banking – Cryptocurrency. June 2018.[2]

themes as to where adoption has taken hold more quickly. Countries where there are higher levels of distrust or corruption in their government are at the top on the list. Also, nations experiencing high inflation and capital control implementations are more likely to see a larger percentage of adopters. In these cases, cryptocurrencies are seen as an escape route from financial repression and wealth confiscation. Users in these countries see blockchain-based assets as trustworthy, useful, and universal (Figure 10.1).

Countries all over the world are recognizing cryptocurrencies as a legitimate financial tool and some have passed laws to permit their usage as legal tender. Yet one of the most exciting points is that even in countries with the widest acceptance, there is still relatively low penetration and lots of room to grow (Figure 10.2)!

FIGURE 10.2 Graphic Depicting Results from the ING International Survey on Mobile Banking

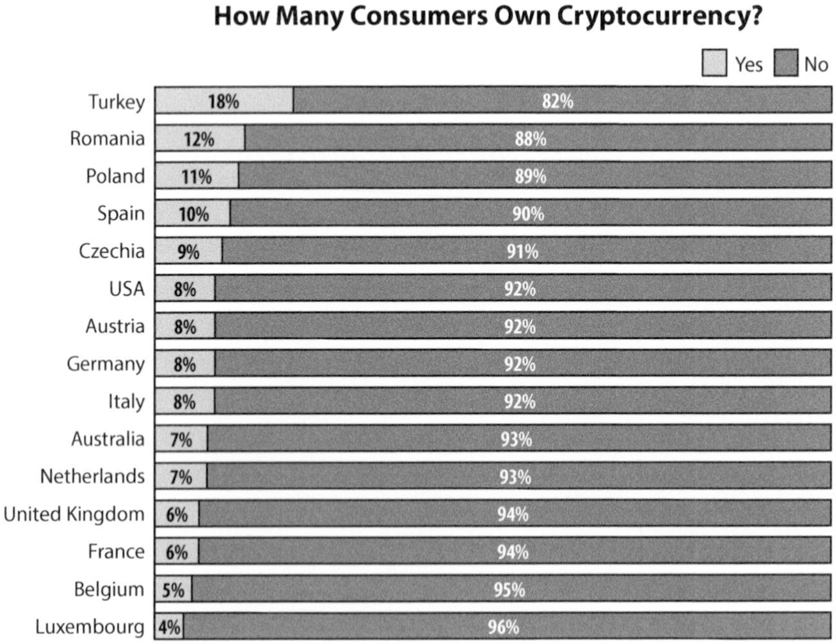

How Many Consumers Own Cryptocurrency?

Source: ING International Survey Mobile Banking – Cryptocurrency, June 2018.[2]

Historical Perspective: Internet Adoption

One of the best ways to get an idea as to how people around the globe will open up to the idea of digital securities is to take some insights from what it took for the world wide web to grow. So how many years did it take for the internet to unfold? In the beginning, the first developments relating to the internet were commissioned by the US government in the 1960s as a way to decentralize their computer systems. The idea was to prevent the military's communication networks from being disrupted if there was an attack on one or more of their locations by an enemy force. This project was taken to a whole new level in the 1980s as additional resources from the various branches of the Armed Forces and multiple universities developed ARPANET as the backbone of most military and academic computer networks in the United States. By the mid-1990s, internet-based technologies were in use in multiple commercial applications.[7]

From an individual user standpoint, though, the global internet we think of today really saw its genesis in 1985 with the establishment of the Domain Name System. By translating numeric IP addresses into alphabetic, easier-to-remember web addresses, this protocol created the ".com," ".org," and other top-level domain formats that we use today. To illustrate, the website "*198.105.232.4*" could instead be called up by "www.example.com." This made it simpler for consumers and average citizens to access and understand the "information superhighway."[8] Earlier adopters and enthusiasts began taking a liking to this new internet phenomenon for a variety of purposes and got connected. By late 1997, various media outlets declared that America Online, the largest internet gateway service at the time, had "conquered cyberspace" by passing the milestone of 10 million subscribers. As internet speeds, content, and affordability increased, so too did the number of people using the web – the growth rate was exponential.

From what it appears, cryptocurrencies are taking hold of the public in a similar way. If internet adoption was measured by how many people were connecting to the web, blockchain adoption might be gauged by how many people have acquired digital wallets. The parallels are quite striking.

It took the internet roughly a dozen years to reach 10 million users. Bitcoin's initial release was in January 2009; according to Statista, there were over 30 million Bitcoin wallet holders just ten years later (and this figure doesn't even count if other cryptocurrency wallets are being used!). New customers on crypto exchanges are picking up exponentially. If the internet's historical path is any guide into what will happen in the future, the usage growth of cryptocurrencies should continue to explode. (See Figure 10.3.)

FIGURE 10.3   Comparing Growth of the Internet & Crypto Usage

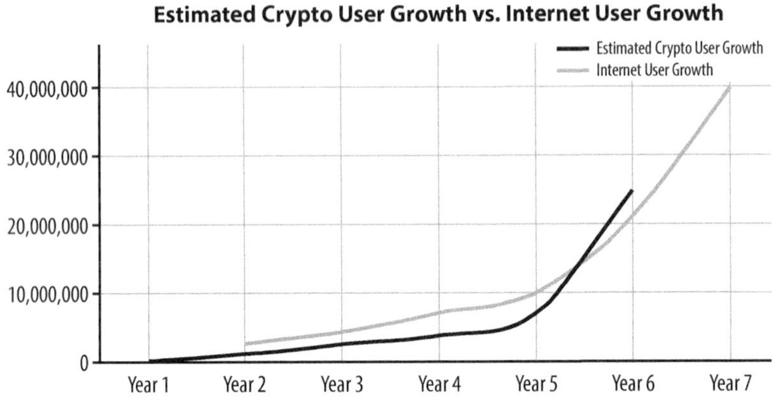

Estimated Crypto User Growth vs. Internet User Growth

Source: Blockchain.info, Medium[9,10]

Case Study: FIO Protocol & The Foundation for Interwallet Operability

If you are really happy as a result of reading my book or you for some reason are feeling very generous today, might I recommend you sending me some Bitcoin? If you are interested, you can send some to my wallet address:

3EypPbo2LvAhDYfnjUyLQm2Fa9UdMjZeem

Now before you extend this generosity, let me provide a few notes of caution:

- Make sure the address above is entered exactly right before you send any Bitcoin my way. If you type in the address incorrectly, even by so much as one letter or number, not only will I not get the Bitcoins, but also, the coins will likely be lost somewhere in cyberspace. No one will end up getting them. As there is no central authority governing Bitcoin, there is no one to contact to reverse the transaction and recover what you've lost. Remember these transactions are irreversible and there's no going back!
- Make sure you are sending Bitcoin, *and only Bitcoin*, to this address. If you end up sending another digital security, say Bitcoin Cash or Ethereum, that gift will never get to me and again will probably be lost somewhere in cyberspace.
- If the transaction is indeed successful, I will likely never know it came from you because there are limited mechanisms to attach a message letting me know that you are indeed the sender. So let me apologize upfront that I will never be able to thank you properly for your gift.

   While this is my Bitcoin wallet address at Coinbase, I honestly don't believe anyone will send Bitcoin over – and that is not the real objective of what I'm trying to do in this section. What I am trying to show is just how frightening, risky, and difficult it can be to transfer cryptocurrency and utilize wallets.

One of the most intimidating features of cryptocurrency is the wallet address. Typically, a wallet address is a long combination of letters and numbers. This is extremely complicated and daunting, especially for a new user to cryptocurrency. With all of these problems to navigate, many people are probably asking themselves, "Why am I dealing with cryptocurrency in the first place?"

Fortunately, there is an easier way. The Foundation for Interwallet Operability has partnered with several leading cryptocurrency firms such as Binance to develop the FIO protocol. Instead of long complicated addresses, wallet users can adopt one easy-to-remember FIO wallet address where all cryptocurrencies and digital assets can be sent. FIO addresses utilize the structure of **username@domain** – similar to what we use for email addresses.

On top of that, FIO users can send requests that include messages and invoices directly to other wallets. This eliminates human error while providing ease around the amounts, reasons for transfer, and proper address for handling the cryptocurrency. Using the FIO protocol, all types of data can be sent with these requests; attachments of memos, invoices, or receipts can be included in a format that is easy to store. More and more wallets are now adopting the FIO protocol to securely and efficiently use digital assets.

FIO address provides many other benefits, including:

- Blockchain Agnostic: FIO address should work identically across coins and token platforms. It should not matter if you use Bitcoins, Ethereum, or whatever. This includes being able to update seamlessly with new coins or tokens.
- Wallet Agnostic: FIO users are free to use a plethora of wallet products and are not inclined to operate a specific company's offerings.
- Privacy: While you utilize a unique, easy-to-remember name for your wallet address, the protocol incorporates encryption to limit others' knowledge of your transactions.

Earlier, we discussed how the internet adopted the Domain Name System, or DNS, in 1985, allowing easier-to-remember web addresses. With DNS, the website "198.105.232.4" could instead be called up by "www.example.com." The FIO protocol should create a similar type of effect with cryptocurrencies and digital assets, thus fostering increased adoption of wallet products and services.

Now before moving on, let me just give you one other option if for some reason you are still interested in sending me a digital gift. If you have a FIO-enabled wallet, you can send me something here instead:

BAXTER@EDGE

This address accepts many types of digital assets, including Bitcoin, Ethereum, Chainlink, Tether, USDCoin, and many others! And if you do want a "Thank

(continued)

(continued)

You," just include your name and contact info in a memo and I'll be sure to get back to you shortly!

– P.S. Hopefully, I have now proved my point that it is much easier to deal in digital transactions in this manner!

"Crypto payments must improve if this technology is going to expand. FIO's approach, decentralized, cross-chain, and with financial incentives to adopt, is exciting and we're thrilled to support it."

Erik Voorhees, Founder and CEO of ShapeShift[11]

"Normalizing the use of human-readable addresses is paramount to achieving long-term, mass adoption of blockchain. We are proud to work alongside FIO to push for mainstream accessibility of this technology and work toward a decentralized future that everyone can partake in with zero learning curve."

Maxim Blagov, CEO of Enjin[11]

The Next Wave of Users

So what will it take for digitized assets to hit the mainstream? Digital assets will likely first get picked up by those who face high banking costs or in locations where financial systems are nonexistent or less than efficient. But digital products should also find favor from those most sophisticated in their knowledge of technology and investing.

Millennials

Globally, Millennials are a blockbuster demographic and represent 2.6 billion people who grew up with the internet and have an affinity for technology. As a result, this generation has been more likely to experiment with and adopt new trends. Cryptocurrency and blockchain-based applications have been no exception.

In 2016, Facebook commissioned a study that surveyed over 25,000 people and collected data from the Facebook conversations of another 70 million users. The participants aged anywhere from 21 to 34. The purpose of the study was to better understand the financial habits of the Millennial generation. The findings were broad – one underlying theme though was that Millennials have an aversion to financial companies and banks in general. To be more specific, 92% of those surveyed expressed distrust for banks – and roughly a third stated that they didn't believe they would need a bank in five years.[12,13] Perhaps more surprisingly, another study observed that just over 70% said they would rather go into a dentist office than go into a branch of a bank![14] Young adults clearly would like to find an alternative way handle their money. Digital securities seem to be a natural fit!

Institutional Investors

Institutional investors can be thought of as the "big boys" or "gorillas on the block" of Wall Street. This would include groups that might manage funds for pension plans, endowments, foundations, universities, or sovereign wealth funds. These firms usually have the additional means and sophisticated knowledge that provides them access to a variety of investment options that usually would not be open to the general public.

Several large, well-known institutions have expressed interest in the idea of investing in digital assets. Given the incredible returns that cryptocurrencies like Bitcoin generated over the past decade, even a small allocation to digital assets could have had a meaningful increase in the overall profits of these organizations. At this point in time, many pension plans and other organizations are experiencing intense pressures because they are underfunded. The need to squeeze out costs, increase investment opportunities, and enhance returns has never been so great.

But today there are several obstacles that prevent the adoption of digital tokens. The biggest hurdle may be custody requirements. Laws typically require that assets managed by institutions be held by a qualified custodial bank that can provide safeguarding and other specialized financial services. The custody of digital assets, particularly cryptocurrencies, can be a bit tricky. Until all the kinks in the custodial process are worked out, institutions may refrain from entering the space. In June 2019, Greenwich Associates released a report that surveyed a number of leaders in the financial space. These executives expressed that a "lack of regulatory clarity" was the top impediment to security token adoption.[15] As these issues continue to be sorted out, institutions may be eagerly waiting on the sidelines.

Hurdles for Tokenization

Academic research has shown that people are more likely to gravitate toward products or services that are tangible and familiar. As a result, security tokens that are backed by something such as gold, shares of a Fortune 500 company, or a trophy real estate property likely will prove to be suitable. However, there are also a few other major concerns that investors should consider in regard to privacy and safety around the blockchain itself.

Privacy

For various reasons, people may want to maintain an element of anonymity regarding the size of positions they have or their trading activity pertaining to their investment holdings. There are certain people who simply are private and do not want others to know their business; then there are those who may want to keep information to themselves in order to prevent others from taking advantage. Some security issuers will not want to have their securities tokens traded on a platform for everyone to see nor will they want the tokens to be available to just any individual. As a result, you may find some projects gravitating toward private blockchains that will only allow permissioned investors to trade. Whatever the reason may be, until a solution to such privacy issues is determined, current methods employed on blockchains may not be suitable for certain markets.

Suppose you had the wealth of Bill Gates. What do you think would happen to the price of a piece of land that you expressed interest in? The owners would likely start seeing dollar signs flash in their heads and immediately jack up their opinion of what the land was worth. On the other hand, suppose you wanted to sell your massive stake in a company like Microsoft. If the market got wind of this, some would start selling as well in order to get out of the way of the potential flood of shares that were about to enter the market. Buyers would become wery of the investment in light of a big owner getting rid of such a large position. Lack of privacy would hinder your own liquidity! The same could be true if the market noticed a highly valued account on a blockchain moving its weight around.

There are solutions on the market today that can help with issues around privacy. Digital identities can be linked to multiple accounts or wallets and be kept secret from other users on the chain. Proper infrastructure though will be needed to make this happen. As of yet, there doesn't seem to be a commonly accepted standard on how to do this. Until this question is answered, people will shy away from using security tokens.

Quantum Computing

Quantum computing would be a major breakthrough for our society in that it would allow the computational speed of machines to increase by an exponential magnitude as compared to what we have now. Quantum computing operates at the subatomic level (the things that actually make up an individual atom) and this allows for physical properties that are far more sophisticated and robust than what standard machines function on today.

Because of the mindblowing speeds at which these machines compute, the cryptography that serves as the backbone to blockchains could be compromised. Quantum computers would theoretically have the strength to break or decode most of the password protections mechanisms we use today. With quantum computing, it may be possible for someone to determine a password very quickly and thus gain access to any token wallet or account.

Keep in mind that this would not just be a threat for blockchain; rather it would be a challenge to just about all computer infrastructure. Our email systems, credit card networks, social media, and internet commerce rely on encryption techniques that would be vulnerable.

But quantum computing needs several more years of testing before it becomes a real threat. The most powerful machines utilized by IBM and Google are up to about 50 qubits (the basic unit of quantum computing) – many experts believe a quantum computer would need about 1,500 qubits to crack Bitcoin's cryptographic functions.[16] Quantum computing is difficult to achieve because it requires extremely sophisticated hardware and requires low temperatures that are almost physically impossible to simulate and maintain for long periods of time.

Cryptography has always been about making the security around a system too time intensive and costly to crack. Steps could be taken to increase that security very quickly if quantum computers posed a problem. Blockchains could be upgraded with additional layers of protection. Also, password managers are fairly common today. These apps could take additional measures to ensure private keys and passwords are not in harm's way. Thus, we should be able to outsource our needs to experts who have a vested interest in making sure everyone stays safe. In conclusion, we should have ample solutions in place by the time quantum computers are a real threat.

Case Study: COVID-19 – The Novel Coronavirus and the Need for Blockchain Solutions

> "I think this is an opportunity for a move to digital. I believe this crisis will accelerate and move people to utilize all forms of digital financial services."
>
> Peter Gordon, President of Emerging Payments at U.S. Bank[17]

The outbreak of the novel coronavirus in early 2020 caused shockwaves throughout our planet. The "COVID-19" pandemic would set about an unprecedented human, health, and economic crisis the likes of which the modern world had never seen. This virus forced hundreds of millions in over 100 countries to "Stay at Home" or "Shelter in Place" and kept people from all walks of life from going to schools, traveling to their places of work, and meeting up in their spaces of common gathering. The impact was severe, pressing, and unavoidable for all.

After the advent of the outbreak, asset prices fell sharply. At its worst points, the selloff resulted in declines that rivaled those of the Global Financial Crisis of 2008. Stresses showed up in funding markets and credit spreads jumped like never before. As the market volatility spiked, liquidity deteriorated, and global exchanges were left in a state of utter panic. The world's economies had to brace themselves on the fears of an upcoming deep recession, or even depression.

These moments exposed the fragility of our global economic system. With people incapable of going to work and goods unable to move freely, our supply

(continued)

(continued)

chains were impacted and the monetary engine that once moved about so easily before the pandemic began to sputter. With capital practically frozen, financial firms were put into a distressed situation and millions of people – seemingly overnight – were forced out of their jobs. Questions arose as to whether basic payments of salaries, mortgages, rents, or loans would or even could be made. This uncertainty caused a dramatic change in people's behavior. Many unthinkable events happened and shook our economic reality to its core, for example:

- The Philippine Stock Exchange halted all trading operations in mid-March of 2020 for a two-day stretch.[18]
- The Depository Trust Company (DTC) suspended all efforts to process paper-based certificates for several weeks.[19]
- Retail bank branches closed their doors in fear of contagion.[20]

As happens in all times of economic calamity, people looked to the various governmental authorities – local, state, and national – as well as our largest financial institutions to provide solutions. Indeed, governments quickly passed legislation allowing for stimulus and relief. But questions came up as to whether the actual legislated measures could be implemented quickly enough to subside the damage that was unfolding.

In the United States, the federal government decided to provide payments of $1,200 to qualifying individuals as a way to put money in people's pockets. These funds would provide temporary relief to people who had lost their jobs or seen their wealth deteriorate as a result of the crisis. It was intended as a way for people to have cash to purchase basic necessities and meet their obligations such as rent. The Treasury Department was instructed to make payments as swift as possible to counter the pain people were feeling and to provide hope for struggling businesses. Unfortunately, numerous glitches showed up in the system that prevented a seamless rollout. Examples included:

- Many citizens had difficulties receiving and/or cashing their checks.
- Millions who filed taxes with popular services such as H&R Block or Turbo Tax did not have their direct deposit information on file.
- A number of people received the wrong amount of money.
- Fraudsters looked to wrongfully claim benefits.
- Some looking for an update about their payment on the IRS website received the message "Payment Status Not Available."

There were likely numerous other problems and glitches that occurred during this period. According to the *Washington Post*, only half of the 150 million payments that were expected under the "Economic Impact Payment" program were actually completed in the first three weeks.[21] The coronavirus was first and foremost a human tragedy; regardless of what or how things went wrong, society was forced to consider whether or not it was optimizing the efforts to handle such a situation. This led to the question, "Could digital currencies provide a better path forward?"

In the United States, two bills were brought to the floor of the House of Representatives detailing the idea of a national digital currency. Leaders such as Senator Sherrod Brown of Ohio discussed a digitized version of the existing dollar[22] and documents showed that a similar discussion was had among the Council of the European Union for a digital euro.[23] International organizations brought the idea of digitizing currencies to light as well.

> "The pandemic may hence put calls for CBDCs (Central Bank Digital Currencies) into sharper focus, highlighting the value of having access to diverse means of payments, and the need for any means of payments to be resilient against a broad range of threats."
> Excerpt from the Bank of International Settlements' April 3, 2020 Bulletin[24]

A digital euro or digital dollar will exhibit far less friction than the ones we use today. The COVID-19 lockdown was a time when people needed cash right away and the speed and ease of its use was paramount. Why should hundreds of millions of people have to wait extra days to receive their money just so that banks and clearinghouses can credit their accounts? Why would our society continue to accept this slowdown especially when a better solution exists and the need for a replacement is so pressing? Why should those who are unbanked have to suffer the costs of using high-priced check cashing services when cheaper methods are available? Digital currencies can help mitigate risk and lead to a more stable economic existence. Adopting a digital form of payment can help to diversify our society into new ways of doing business. Other problems will likely be alleviated as well – digital currencies can lead to less money laundering, help to eliminate fraud, and stop counterfeiting. It seems like now is the time to really bring the debates about digital currencies to a head and determine if it is time to move forward with a new electronic method of payment.

Other blockchain applications were discussed to tackle problems stemming from the coronavirus. Countries like the United Arab Emirates used blockchain and digital identity to step up their fight in combating the coronavirus. The Middle Eastern nation established goals that set about programs that would allow its citizens to access government services remotely rather than having to visit physical offices and service centers.[25] Innovative companies like Ant Financial took measures to assist its clientele. Electronic vouchers were disseminated via Alipay as a way to boost consumer spending. Ant Financial and its subsidiary

(continued)

(continued)

MYbank amplified its programs to provide loans through mobile applications. Their lending apps provided a way to grant loans in as little as three minutes with zero manual intervention. These "contactless" loans were intended to support almost ten million small and medium-sized enterprises, individual businesses, and farmers across China. This solution was ideal as so many people were forced to remain in isolation during the lockdowns.

> "The service sector in China is still in the nascent stages of digital transformation, and that means it has huge untapped potential. Amid the ongoing coronavirus outbreak, we have also seen how digital technology can be used to help service providers become more agile and respond effectively to the fast-changing market environment."
> Simon Hu, Chief Executive Officer of Ant Financial[26]

History will likely look back at the COVID-19 crisis as a pivotal moment in the progression of digital solutions. Blockchain applications are now being closely examined as a new way of doing things by people in the highest seats of power. Digital Fintech companies showed they were more geared to working remotely and that they were able to provide services without customer disruption. Stablecoins and smart contracts proved themselves to be powerful tools to mitigate risk. It appears that the crisis opened society's eyes to the need for constant financial evolution, and that going digital can be a viable path for the future.

Fintech companies, though, must not be so eager as to pounce too quickly at this opportunity. The crisis has a human side and its emotional elements must be handled appropriately. Furthermore, leaders in the digital field must be careful not to overpromise – it is paramount to maintain a level-headed approach. While blockchain has so much to offer, there is still room for implementation error. Rushing solutions through could lead to missteps that could be detrimental in the long run.

Some additional interest events that occurred during the COVID-19 pandemic:

Despite dropping rapidly in value at the onset of the pandemic, cryptocurrencies like Bitcoin and Ethereum recovered much of their losses quickly – both were once again trading with year-to-date gains by mid-April 2020. Global stocks could not say the same. Volumes on cryptocurrency exchanges hit new highs.[27,28,29]

Demand for stablecoins increased dramatically as money poured into popular venues like Tether and USDCoin.[30,31]

Retailers like Publix, Lidl, and Bi-Lo started to accept contactless payments as cash was seen as a potential avenue for transmitting germs.[32]

The US Department of Homeland Security deemed Blockchain Managers as a "Critical Service."[33]

Blockchain companies such as Paxos, BlockFi, Coin Desk, and eToro continued to hire employees throughout the crisis as demand for their services continued.[34,35]

Chapter Summary

- As digital solutions obtain better features and functionality, the number of users should increase at a brisk rate for the foreseeable future.
- Cryptocurrency is the typical gateway people use to first experience digital financial products. One of the initial steps that has to be taken anytime a new user gets accustomed to using cryptocurrency is to first acquire a digital wallet.
- Millennials, with their affinity for technology, seem to be a group ripe for adopting digital solutions like security tokens.
- Additional work needs to be done with blockchain-based securities in terms of both privacy and safety. Quantum computing poses a threat not only to blockchain but to our entire online infrastructure – additional layers of protection will be needed from these super-fast machines. Quantum breakthroughs are not likely for at least a few more years.
- Recent events such as the COVID-19 pandemic will accelerate the adoption of blockchain technology and digital assets.

CONCLUDING THOUGHTS

- Education will be key for blockchain adoption.
- Today's blockchain leaders may or may not maintain their status as time passes.
- Digitization alone is not enough – projects need strong underlying economics to succeed.

Need for Education

In order for security tokens to seriously take root, grow, and flourish, the market and all of its constituents need to be further educated. Security token usage will be a growing trend in the market; but to realize their full potential, there are still a lot of terms and concepts that the general public will need to absorb and understand; these terms can be confusing and the ideas difficult to grasp. This goes not only for retail investors but also for people employed in the financial industry, market regulators, and entrepreneurs trying to issue securities to raise capital.

What makes security tokens so appealing to the investment industry is the technologically advanced breakthroughs. Ironically, it is this same technology factor, and the fear thereof, that is causing the industry to tap the brakes on adoption. In writing this book, I have consistently found myself looking for ways to go into less detail about the technology because this discussion can confuse and scare people away from embracing this exciting opportunity. Eventually people will see first-hand the value that others, who moved before them, are getting by having made the transition – and perhaps then they too will make the switch. But we have yet to see an inflection point in acceptance, and until then, a more grassroots approach will have to be taken.

To best persuade people to get involved with digital securities, the public will have to be convinced that tokens are not a scary thing and that they are actually better for them. Fintech companies will have to look for ways to take the technology away from the interface and make every interaction simpler and user friendly. The easier these products are to use and the fewer steps that have to be taken to acquire them, the faster the adoption rates will be.

The education around the infrastructure of digital assets and security tokens will need to move its focus to the end result: from switching over to blockchain technology rather than the details of the actual intricacies of the technology. Those working to promote this industry and attract a customer base will need to reframe their marketing narratives toward discussing the benefits these tokens provide. If you tell a financial firm, "I know a way to save you a tremendous amount of money on the settlement of your trades and on your firm's back office costs," people's ears will perk up. If you say to an entrepreneur looking to fund a new project, "Have you heard about this new thing issuers are doing to lower their cost of capital and shorten time to market?," that will cause excitement and at least grab a few minutes of her attention span. This approach of leading with cost savings and efficiency gains tends to work better than starting up a lecture on how blockchain works or defining a security token.

But what else can be done? At this point in time, the two biggest issues for faster uptake are around custody and the safety of wallets. If the industry could get a better grasp around these two issues, you may see a greater level of acceptance.

Unfortunately, at this point in the game, those with the best access to tokenized securities are only accredited investors. In order for someone to meet the criteria of an accredited investor, they usually have to have a certain amount of net worth or income. Strangely, these people are statistically most likely to be in an older age demographic and are less likely to have grown up around technology. As a result, digital wallets are an unsettling topic and the concept of custody could be confusing. This creates a hurdle to adoption and forces more handholding.

People will need to become more accustomed to dealing with digital wallets. Even if the ways in which these wallets are used are simple and do not contain sophisticated investment products, merely their initial usage will be a big step forward for many individuals. Once people start to familiarize themselves with wallets and their subsequent benefits, they will be more likely to take further strides from there.

Mostly due to regulatory hurdles, institutional investors have been hesitant to really push their leadership, management, and beneficiaries to take a good hard look at digital assets. Even if they could get buy-in from their stakeholders, regulators may still not allow them to do anything in the space due to custodial issues. But some institutional players are continuing to explore ways to deal with the new risks involved. Once the custody questions are resolved, institutional interest will likely explode.

It is incredibly exciting to see the progress that the security token industry has made. Without many formal ways of getting up to speed on the exciting developments that are unfolding, people are still managing to keep abreast of what is happening. Much of this self-education has been fueled by intellectual curiosity and a passion for the potential that this technological breakthrough can make.

As I have spoken with people over the years about the possibilities of digital securities, time and time again I have seen people start off being very skeptical of what I tell them. But it seems almost like clockwork that gradually, peoples' interest gets piqued as they hear more about it. After not too long, these same folks become fully engaged and are fully attentive to the possibilities that the digitization of securities will bring!

Industry Trends – Creating a Cashless Society: The Rise of Mobile Payments in Asia

Mobile payment usage has been on the rise worldwide for some time. Advances in smartphone technology have made payment services available to anyone, anywhere, anytime with just a swipe of the finger or the tap of the screen. A study by PwC found that almost one-third of consumers globally paid for purchases using their mobile phone during in-store shopping experiences.[1] Payment platforms such as Apple Pay, PayPal, WeChat, and Alipay boast active users in the hundreds of millions and this number is rising briskly. Both consumers and vendors are finding mobile payments to be a cheaper and more convenient method in which to conduct business – in fact, many consumers have come to expect mobile payments as an option when purchasing goods or services.

But there is a wide variation of adoption rates in this form of commerce from country to country. Today, Asia is clearly at the forefront of this major trend and the region is seeing a dramatic uptick in the percentage of transactions that are taking place literally at the consumers' fingertips. In 2018, China's mobile payment market grew 58% and was worth nearly $28 trillion. Today, roughly 86% of the population in China is making mobile payment transactions through apps such as Alipay or WeChat Pay.[1] Other Asian nations are following suit. Both Thailand and Vietnam are now seeing over 60% of their consumers using their smartphones when making purchases.[2] In fact, the government of Vietnam has a plan for the country to be cashless by 2027.[3] Today, eight of the world's top 10 mobile payment nations are in Asia and growth rates in the region are significantly higher than in the rest of the world.

> "Asia remains the powerhouse in leading the customer shift to mobile payments with the report reflecting eight Asian nations in the top 10, and six are in Southeast Asia. Vietnam, with its relatively low penetration in 2018, has registered the highest growth as mobile platforms demonstrate a significant increase in convenience over traditional means of commerce."
>
> Shirish Jain, Director of PwC's Strategy & Payments Division[4]

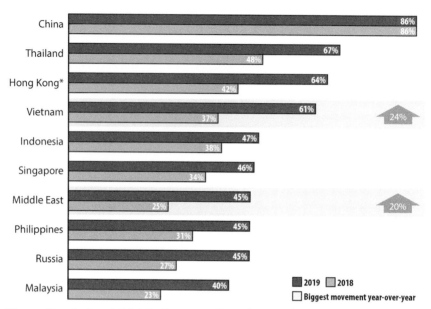

Figure Conclusion.1 Mobile Payment Growth Rates by Country Source: PwC Global Consumer Insights Survey, 2019[5]

One extremely exciting byproduct of this trend toward mobile payments is the fact that it is bringing people who were once unbanked into the global financial ecosystem. China, India, Pakistan, and Indonesia rank at the top of the list of nations with the largest populations of people without a traditional bank account. The adoption of mobile payments in these places is clearly accelerating financial inclusion and according to the World Bank, having access to a mobile money provider or platform is a crucial step in escaping poverty.

The payment industry is buoyed by many factors, one of which is blockchain technology. In order for this area to continue to thrive and function at an instantaneous and trouble-free level, payments need the proper mechanisms to facilitate the transferring of data between banks and other industry participants. It should come as no surprise that the leading firms in payment technologies are also the most prolific filers of patents in blockchain. Chinese tech giants Tencent and Alibaba, the companies behind WeChat Pay and Alipay respectively, accounted for more than 1,000 blockchain patents combined in 2019. Clearly, these world leaders are turning to distributed ledger technology to solidify their positions and expand market shares in this rapidly expanding field. Blockchain seems ideal in this use case as it provides low cost, transparent, secure, and inclusive financial services to individuals and small business globally. It is likely that the technology will be used even more extensively as time goes on.

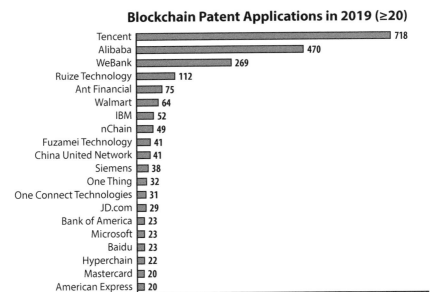

Figure Conclusion.2 Blockchain Patent Applications by Company Source: Google Patents, The Block[6]

Ant Financial

Ant Financial Services is an affiliate company of the well-known Chinese firm Alibaba Group. Ant Financial is best known for operating Alipay, the world's largest mobile and online payments platform. Today, Alipay reaches over 1 billion people worldwide and this number is expected to double within the next 10 years. This incredible reach makes Alipay the world's most used app outside of those in social networking. With its massive customer base and innovative leadership, Ant Financial is disrupting the Asian financial system and these ripples are being felt worldwide.

Ant Financial's products and services are so useful that they are now a vital part of daily life in China. Credit Suisse estimates that nearly 60% of all online payments circulate through Alipay! While some people still think of the company simply for its platform Alipay, Ant Financial has grown to much more than just a payment gateway. Ant owns subsidies in asset management, credit scoring, micro-financing and technology services. Mobile clients have parked more than $150 billion in the company's flagship money mutual fund known as Tianhong Yu'e Bao – roughly one-third of all Chinese people have deposits there![7] Based on just this insight alone it is easy to see how much of a juggernaut Ant Financial has become.

Not just confined to China, Ant Financial is also making tremendous inroads with its overseas expansion plans. Alipay works with over 250 international financial institutions and supports more than 25 currencies. As China's middle class grows and its citizens travel more abroad, non-Chinese firms have been eager to utilize Alipay. These factors only contribute to Ant Financial's forward march toward becoming a global payments powerhouse. In the last few years, the number of merchants in Europe that accept Alipay has tripled and Ant Financial has created partnerships with various European digital wallet apps such as ePassi (Finland), Vipps (Norway), MOMO (Spain), Pagaqui (Portugal), and Bluecode (Austria). In March 2019, Barclaycard expanded an agreement with Ant Financial that enabled British retailers to take Alipay in their stores. Ant Financial has also made steps to successfully expand its business into the United States, India, and Southeast Asia.[8]

The key to Ant Financial's staggering success is its commitment to innovation and technological leadership. The company is clearly a model for how to use technology and create product and services that consumers find useful, necessary, and competitive.

"Ant is about building tech and putting it into the right places to achieve scale in financial services."

Eric Jing, Executive Chairman Ant Financial[9]

What has been so impressive about Ant's technology development relates to how it interfaces with its clients. Ant has been able to use blockchain in many ways – there are times when the product they deliver deliberately markets itself as utilizing blockchain; other times, the blockchain technology is simply in the background and totally kept out of the user's mind. This two-pronged approach is a very smart and necessary way to deliver the benefits of blockchain.

Let's take an example where blockchain is kept behind the curtain. In the case of a standard Alipay transaction, the client does not need to know all of the inner workings of what is going on to facilitate the processing and moving of money from one party to another. The customer's concerns are simply around the reliability, safety, and efficiency of the payment. So long as everything is done properly, those users will be happy. When it comes to interacting with a service or a function, one is not concerned with everything behind the curtain, just that the function occurs as promised. Think of this in the same way as when you might go to get a cup of water from your sink. You don't need or necessarily want to know where the water came from, how it was purified, or what pipes it came through to get to your home. You just need to know that when you turn your faucet on, clean water will come out – all other details are unnecessary.

On the other hand, there are times the customer does need to know more about the technology. Take the case when Ant launched its "Blockchain Open Alliance," an enterprise blockchain platform for small businesses. The purpose of this initiative was to enable small-scale and micro-enterprises to develop their own blockchain applications with low costs and limited time commitment. Alipay's clients could leverage what Ant Financial had already built to improve their businesses. This program led to the development of food tracking, healthcare, and agri-product monitoring apps that used blockchain. In this case, Ant feels it can best service its customers by opening up its platform so that customers can better tap demands. If these customers succeed, Ant will thus enhance Alipay's distribution efficiency.[10]

> "In the past two years, Ant Financial has been working on two aspects about blockchain. One is to improve the technology, and the other is to open it up and accelerate the commercialization of blockchain applications."
> Jiang Guofei, President of Ant Financial's Smart Technology Group[11]

Ant Financial has successfully taken blockchain to the marketplace through both of these avenues. The company has utilized very smart and effective marketing to push blockchain to the masses. This has been highly beneficial to Ant Financial and to the Chinese society as a whole. It is also a reason why Asian countries are so far ahead of countries in the West in terms of harnessing and utilizing this transformational technology to their benefit.

Who Will Succeed in This Race for Blockchain Dominance – Notes of Caution

> Steve Jobs: "We're better than you are! We have better stuff."
> Bill Gates: "You don't get it, Steve. That doesn't matter!"
> —Excerpt from the 1999 movie, "Pirates of Silicon Valley"[12]

The concept of the first mover advantage is quite simple, regardless of the product or market: the firm that first delivers a product in a new market space is likely to distinguish itself as the industry standard, gain brand recognition, and have a size advantage over new entrants. The resulting customers stay loyal and provide revenues that can be used for continued growth. As the number of users of the product increases, scale and the cost of switching platforms can increase. The first mover firm is then rewarded with near-monopoly status and high returns.

Keep in mind that this concept is more of a guideline than a rule. While technology firms often do see an advantage if they can move quickly and before others there are often instances where the incumbent provider becomes bogged down in its initial niche and is unable to meet the demands of a changing market.

Historical Perspectives: First Mover Advantages

MySpace (and to a lesser extent, Friendster) was the first significant player in social media. It attracted a tremendous number of people who used its website and built their own social media pages. However, Facebook was able to come in much later and provide a new and better product for a different generation, whose tastes were different and whose worldview was more technologically savvy.[13] Facebook grew tremendously as younger clientele were more likely to gravitate toward the hipper, more cutting-edge platform. MySpace was put into a dilemma – stay the course with its established user base or reengineer its website to go after the broader market. The first option had limited potential; the second one was extremely risky. If MySpace rolled out a new format, it likely would have angered its current users who were familiar with its navigation and functionality. Also, there was no guarantee current or new customers would accept the new design. This is why flexibility and superior design are key at the time of product launch. It is often too difficult to "rebuild the plane while it is in mid-flight"!

In order to pull off a first mover advantage successfully for the long term, the product has to provide a hands-down, strong competitive advantage in its industry or otherwise clearly differentiate itself from its competitors.

The digital financial marketplace is still in its infancy. In many cases, products that were first to market have tended to maintain their dominant market share and premium valuations. Bitcoin continues to be the dominant cryptocurrency and Tether continues to be the dominant stablecoin; this is most likely due to the first mover advantage each had in its respective product line. Trading volumes and trading liquidity are crucial for successfully functioning markets and the network effect of having an established, loyal user base has seemingly kept these two products firmly entrenched in their top market positions.

In the stablecoin market, there are several offerings that, in my opinion, have stronger fundamentals than Tether. This is because Tether has the following weaknesses:

Questionable Reserves: Tether formerly stated that each token was backed 1:1 with US dollars. But in March 2019, this claim was altered to include the backing of loans to affiliate companies. This drew into question if Tether Limited, the organization that coordinates Tether, had adequate reserves and if those reserves' valuations were subject to changes in market conditions. Also, Tether Limited has failed to provide promised audited financial statements in regard to its reserves.[14]

Redemption Policy: Tether Limited states that owners of Tethers have no legal rights or guarantees that Tethers can be exchanged or redeemed for dollars.

These factors led to Tether's traded price dropping below its theoretical value of $1 on several occasions.[15] One of the main selling points of blockchain is that it should enhance trust. As should be done when investing in any coin or token, read the offering document and look for red flags like unaudited assets or those assets that are not custodied with a credible third party.

At the time of this writing, there are other stablecoins that appear to have sounder operating policies and more transparent reporting. Should the markets be placed under periods of intense stress, Tether's position as the go-to stablecoin may once again come under pressure. Switching costs in the stablecoin market are relatively low and market participants likely would not severely penalize others who used a product other than Tether.

Bitcoin has by far the largest market capitalization of all cryptocurrencies[16] as it is head-and-shoulders better known globally than the other cryptocurrencies. As the first mover to market, Bitcoin began as a standalone cryptocurrency and generally is considered to have weaker technological features than that of other cryptocurrencies. Bitcoin has been able though to gain faith in the market with innovations such as the Lightning Network that is reported to increase its transaction speed and throughput.[17]

The jury is still out as to whether Bitcoin can retain the "digital gold" status it enjoys now. As it is not backed by any other assets and its technology, at this point in time, has not shown comparability with others on the market, Bitcoin will have to continue to rely on its brand name and network effects to drive value and warrant its position in the digital economy.

Big Fish, Little Fish, and the Mighty Whales

"There are big fish and there are little fish, but we like to think we are a fast fish!"
Ed Tuohy, CEO of MERJ Exchange Limited – the world's first company to publicly list a security token on a national stock exchange[18]

There's no doubt about it – big corporations have taken notice of what blockchain and security tokens can do for the financial industry. Not only do they know it, but also, they are taking action. In earlier chapters, moves being made by Facebook's consortium, Walmart, Fidelity, and others were discussed. Goldman Sachs, JPMorgan Chase, and similar banks are adopting blockchain to run portions of their back office. Service providers like Reuters and Bloomberg are seeking to build their datafeeds and information systems to keep their readers informed about how the blockchain industry unfolds. Accounting giants like Pricewaterhouse Coopers and Grant Thornton are now providing audit and consulting business to the digital space. The list goes on and on. C-Suite executives know the potential this new technology holds and the risks of ignoring the inevitable are substantial. With tremendous brand power, personnel, and resources at their disposal, mega-firms should have a decided advantage over the start-up Fintech players – at least on paper.

In my experience, working for a major European financial services firm has both positive and not-so-positive aspects. On the one hand, our company had the distribution reach and staying power that would take start-ups decades to amass. Yet on the other hand, the pace of rolling out certain types of new platforms or ideas could seem quite slow at times. The bureaucracy of a large corporation tends to force the speed of progress down to a very slow creep – only the best of the best managed firms can overcome this. In many cases, the Silicon Valley titans have become so big and commanding that they can choke off innovation. The boardrooms of the Fortune 500 are too often filled with executives who would rather not discuss a problem or opportunity lest they might be seen as unfamiliar or less well-versed than others on the subjects. Turf wars, bruised egos, personal vendettas, legacy issues, and the almighty "doing things by the book" are all matters that have to be navigated when attempting to get things done in the corporate world. This can often lead top talent to look to other avenues for career opportunities.

As a result, the smaller competitors in this emerging field have inherently powerful forces behind them. When a market is faced with a transformational event, as is the case in today's financial world with blockchain and security tokens, repeatedly it is the more nimble newcomers who have the willingness and ability to move quickly, adapt to coming changes, and develop cutting-edge offerings tailored to the immediate needs of the market. The mighty and established are often stuck in their ways and too inflexible to meet challenges with the same vigor. Throughout history, consumer adoption of groundbreaking technologies comes about at an exponential rate and it is often the edgier, more pioneering firm that is there to capture the incoming wave of market share.

On top of this, moving into a new venture or market opportunity could have public relations and possible reputational ramifications most executives would like to avoid. In many instances, the big companies know this is a game they simply don't want to play – and in some ways, they don't have to. Large companies typically have a nice luxury in that they can wait – for a limited window of time – to see how things unfold. With their deep pockets, they can then go out and buy the technology, features, and customers the innovative, entrepreneurial firms have obtained. Of course, the terms of negotiation at that point are no longer in their favor.

The point in all this is to realize that nothing is written in stone when it comes to determining who will win out in this upcoming race for digital dominance. It is a new frontier and the rules of the game aren't yet defined. If history is to be our guide, we can see that it would be unwise to count anyone out too early. The past is not necessarily the prologue in the market, however, but may at least provide us with some parameters to look for in determining a winner when all is said and done. Ultimately, it will be the customer who decides.

Historical Perspective: Titans of the Dot-Com Boom, Where Are They Now?

Just because you are in first place today does not guarantee that you will remain there forever. In the mid-1990s, the Information Age was dawning and the internet was a new phenomenon kicking into high gear. Cutting-edge firms released products to stake a claim in this rapidly expanding market. The media and Wall Street divided corporate America into two camps: "new economy" and "old economy." Information technology firms were new economy and everything else was a dinosaur.

Competition was high and successful companies were often richly rewarded in a seemingly winner-take-all environment. This new craze was alluring to investors who were eager to buy stock in a company that might become the next big thing.

America Online: Internet service providers are firms that provide access to the internet. CompuServe and Prodigy were early comers in this field and supplied the mainstream with limited access to the internet and email exchange. Then along came a new would-be juggernaut, America Online, later called AOL. With its catchy "You've Got Mail" slogan and its subscription-based model, America Online turned out to be an unstoppable force on the web. The company became the dominant online service provider internationally and served over 25 million customers in the US.[19]

As time rolled on, cable television companies realized that they had the financing and the inroads with the end customers that were needed to take this market over. AT&T and Verizon began offering internet connections with much higher speeds using broadband technology. Saddled with its dial-up user base, America Online had trouble rebranding itself and finding effective ways to compete in the new regime. AOL and other dial-up providers were left in the dust and today are a shell of their once former glory.

Netscape: Web browsers are software applications that help users to locate and display website pages on the internet. In 1994 when the internet was taking the world by storm, Netscape Navigator was launched and quickly became the most popular web browser. Netscape made an extremely successful IPO in the summer of 1995.[20] The stock was finally set to be offered at a price double what had first been advertised – $28 per share. By the end of its first day of training, the stock closed at nearly $60 per share. Netscape had a market value just shy of $3 billion!

That same year Microsoft threw its hat into the ring by debuting Internet Explorer and a cutthroat "browser war" ensued. Microsoft was able to take the reins and gobble up market share as it was able to bundle Explorer for free with its Windows operating system. Netscape hit back by creating the Mozilla Foundation, which would go on to produce web browser Firefox. Despite all the back-and-forth and struggling, neither Netscape nor Microsoft have been able to hold their once cherished leads in the browser space. Apple Safari has been dominant on Apple platforms since its launch in 2003 and Google Chrome has been dominant elsewhere since 2012.[21,22]

Yahoo!: Web search engines are software systems that allow users to systematically explore content on the internet. As the internet first started getting major traction in American homes, companies like AltaVista, Lycos, Infoseek, and others vied to be the go-to provider for web searches. Yahoo! turned out to be the most popular destination. The company mushroomed in size and went public in 1996.[23] Yahoo! stock would rise on a split adjusted basis from less than $1 at IPO to more than $100 at the height of the dot-com bubble in early 2000. Those same shares would subsequently fall by more than 90% in the next roughly 18 months![24]

By the year 2000, Google was becoming a real force with its smart ranking algorithms that yielded results customers preferred. Web users began gravitating toward Google; the other players learned their search technologies and business models were obsolete and faded away. Today, Google commands over 90% of search engine market share; Yahoo has less than 2%.[25] Fortunately, Yahoo! wisely diversified some of its fortunes from its heyday and made shrewd investments in Yahoo Japan and Alibaba.

Not all of the leaders from this time period, though, went the way of the dodo bird. Eventually the technology sector and the broader economy stabilized. Companies like Amazon, eBay, and Google remained dominant in their respective fields. The dot-com bubble offers some interesting insights into how circumstances can change, often rapidly, in an emerging field. Investors and project managers have to be careful not to get so caught up in the "conventional wisdom" of the day. The internet itself not only survived this period but continued to get bigger and bigger over the next two decades. However, some people who got overly excited got burned when they went all in on the wrong horse! This era reminds us of the importance of due diligence, diversification, and the need for a willingness to change as circumstances dictate.

Never Forget, It's All About the Investment Proposition

The capabilities of security tokens present tremendous benefits for investors. This digitization is positioned to open up new frontiers, strip out costs, create efficiencies, and reduce execution times. Given the potential that security tokens offer over traditional paper certificates, the digital form of ownership should, at the very minimum, be at least equal in value to its paper counterpart. Think about this example – if a baseball team had all of its game stats in a closet full of notebooks, that would be valuable. How much more would this same dataset be worth if all the information were placed in a computer where it was able to be sorted, calculated, and analyzed with the push of a button? This type of incremental usefulness, versatility, and convenience should also be additive for any financial instrument.

Wall Street will always be looking for investment vehicles that combine better contractual flexibility, lower times to market, and the right standing with regulatory authorities. But we should not get so caught up in the excitement of these new possibilities only to forget that investors will always be most interested in the ideas, people, teams, business models, and competitive advantages they are buying. Everything starts with the investment proposition. If the project cannot stand on its own and generate attractive returns, then there's really no reason for anyone to be involved at all. Projects need to produce a high-quality value-adding product or service first and foremost. Period.

If the projects are not good investments from a fundamental standpoint, it will not matter how great the bells and whistles around the technology are. People want to get involved in the underlying asset, not the wrapper. So focus first on the assets that you are buying, how the capital you invest will be deployed, and the people you are partnering with. The technology of digitization behind everything will only make things better!

Conclusion Summary

- Before security tokens can gain mass adoption, education on the topic will be needed.
- Leading players in the blockchain space today may not necessarily remain in this position in the future.
- Small entrepreneurial firms will likely play a critical role in developing security tokens and the new financial market infrastructure.
- Digitization alone is not enough. Projects that are tokenized will also need to have strong underlying business fundamentals in order to succeed.

NOTES

Introduction

1. Sam Volkering, "Is Blockchain the Biggest Opportunity of the Next Decade?", Money Morning, April 7, 2017, https://www.moneymorning.com.au/20170704/blockchain-biggest-opportunity-next-decade.html.

2. Linette Lopez, "How The London Whale Debacle is Partly The Result of an Error Using Excel", Business Insider, February 12, 2013, https://www.businessinsider.com/excel-partly-to-blame-for-trading-loss-2013-2.

3. Peter H. Diamandis and Steven Kotler, "Bold: How to Go Big, Create Wealth and Impact the World" (Simon & Schuster; Reprint Edition, 2016).

Chapter 1. Blockchain Basics

1. "Tyler Winklevoss Quotes", Brainy Quote, Accessed April 1, 2020, https://www.brainyquote.com/quotes/tyler_winklevoss_847146.

2. AXA. "AXA goes blockchain with fizzy". Newsroom. September 13, 2017. https://www.axa.com/en/newsroom/news/axa-goes-blockchain-with-fizzy.

3. Alexandre Clement, "fizzy by AXA: Ethereum Smart Contract in details", Medium, May 24, 2019, https://medium.com/@humanGamepad/fizzy-by-axa-ethereum-smart-contract-in-details-40e140a9c1c0.

4. Rin Kachui, "Why You Should Invest in Learning Blockchain Technology in 2020", APAC Entrepreneur, accessed April 1, 2020, https://apacentrepreneur.com/why-you-should-invest-in-learning-blockchain-technology-in-2020/.

Chapter 2. Fundamentals of a Security Token

1. "FINMA Publishes ICO Guidelines", FINMA, February 16, 2018, https://www.finma.ch/en/news/2018/02/20180216-mm-ico-wegleitung/.

2. Kyle Torpey, " U.S. Lawmakers are Realizing They Can't Ban Bitcoin", Forbes, July 30, 2019, https://www.forbes.com/sites/ktorpey/2019/07/30/us-lawmakers-are-realizing-they-cant-ban-bitcoin/#5cc3326c3e31.

3. "Blockchain Charts", Blockchain.com, accessed April 1, 2020, https://www.blockchain.com/en/charts.

4. "Altcoin News", blokt, accessed April 1, 2020, https://blokt.com/headlines/altcoin.

5. Jeff John Roberts, "Security Tokens Will Be the 'Killer App' of Cryptocurrency, Overstock CEO Says", Fortune, June 20, 2019, https://fortune.com/2019/06/20/security-token-cryptocurrency-overstock-ceo-patrick-byrne/.

6. Nermin Hajdarbegovic, "Chancellor George Osborne has Announced A New Initiative That will Explore the Potential Role of Cryptocurrencies in Britain's Economy.", Coindesk, August 6, 2014, https://www.coindesk.com/george-osborne-unveils-uk-plans-explore-bitcoin.

7. Kate Rooney, "SEC Chief Says Agency Won't Change Securities Laws to Cater to Cryptocurrencies", CNBC, June 6, 2018, https://www.cnbc.com/2018/06/06/sec-chairman-clayton-says-agency-wont-change-definition-of-a-security.html.

8. Paul Vigna, "SEC Clears Blockstack to Hold First Regulated Token Offering", Wall Street Journal, July 10, 2019, https://www.wsj.com/articles/sec-clears-blockstack-to-hold-first-regulated-token-offering-11562794848.

9. Alona Stein, "MERJ Exchange Goes Live With World's First Tokenized IPO", Business Wire, September 12, 2019, https://www.businesswire.com/news/home/20190912005616/en/MERJ-Exchange-Live-World%E2%80%99s-Tokenized-IPO.

10. Wikipedia. "Gold Standard Act". Last modified February 20, 2020. https://en.wikipedia.org/wiki/Gold_Standard_Act.

Chapter 3. What Types of Assets May Be Tokenized?

1. Libra. "Network of Partners". Partners. Accessed April 1, 2020. https://libra.org/en-US/partners/.

2. Rajarshi Mitra, "What is Facebook Libra Cryptocurrency? [The Most Comprehensive Guide]- Part 1", Blockgeeks, accessed April 2, 2020, https://blockgeeks.com/guides/understanding-facebooks-cryptocurrency-libra/.

3. Daniel Roberts, "Facebook's Cryptocurrency Libra Aims to 'Put the Currency Back in Cryptocurrency'", Yahoo!, June 19, 2019, https://finance.yahoo .com/news/facebooks-cryptocurrency-libra-aims-to-put-the-currency-back-in-cryptocurrency-201144888.html.

4. Ron Shevlin, "Why Does Walmart Want a Cryptocurrency", Forbes, August 5, 2019, https://www.forbes.com/sites/ronshevlin/2019/08/05/why-does-walmart-want-a-cryptocurrency/#62c1629c1502.

5. Royal Mint, "Physical Gold Digitally Traded", accessed April 2, 2020, https:// www.royalmint.com/invest/bullion/digital-gold/.

6. Tim Fries, "Aspencoin Transitions to Securitize After Raising $18 Million in Security Token Offering", The Tokenist, September 15, 2019, https:// thetokenist.io/aspencoin-transitions-to-securitize-after-raising-18-million-in-security-token-offering/.

7. Rebecca Campbell, "Securitize to Join IBM's Blockchain Accelerator to Modernize $82T Corporate Debt Market", January 21, 2019, https://www.forbes .com/sites/rebeccacampbell1/2019/01/21/securitize-to-join-ibms-blockchain-accelerator-to-modernize-82t-corporate-debt-market/#11859402486d.

8. "World Bank Issues Second Tranche of Blockchain Bond Via Bond-i", Press Release, The World Bank, August 16, 2019, https://www.worldbank.org/ en/news/press-release/2019/08/16/world-bank-issues-second-tranche-of-blockchain-bond-via-bond-i.

9. Gareth Jenkinson, "Tokenizing Sports – How the Industry is Incorporating Crypto", Cointelegraph, July 28, 2019, https://cointelegraph.com/news/ tokenizing-sports-how-the-industry-is-incorporating-crypto/amp.

10. DREAM Fan Shares LLC. "Fan Shares". About Us. Accessed April 1, 2020, https://dreamfanshares.com/#invest.

11. Michael McCann, "Spencer Dinwiddie and Reimagining the NBA with Tokenized Contracts", Sports Illustrated, November 5, 2019, https://www.si.com/ nba/2019/11/05/spencer-dinwiddie-nets-tokenized-contracts.

12. Benjamin Pirus, "Fatburger and Others Feed $30 Million into Ethereum for New Bond Offering", Forbes, Octiber 9, 2019, https://www.forbes.com/ sites/benjaminpirus/2019/10/09/fatburger-and-others-feed-30-million-into-ethereum-for-new-bond-offering/#29e37f86115b.

13. Michael del Castillo, "Morningstar Rates First Ethereum Security in $40 Million Fatburger Deal", March 8, 2020, https://www.forbes.com/sites/ michaeldelcastillo/2020/03/08/morningstar-rates-first-ethereum-debt-security-in-40-million-fatburger-deal/#3563d5522abd.

14. "iCap Equity Unlocks Liquidity for over $100M in Real Estate Debt Funds using Blockchain-Enabled Harbor Platform", Press Release, PRNewswire, September 16, 2019, https://markets.businessinsider.com/news/stocks/icap-equity-unlocks-liquidity-for-over-100m-in-real-estate-debt-funds-using-blockchain-enabled-harbor-platform-1028527144.

15. Elliot Hill, "Fidelity Creates Blockchain Token to Reward Employees", November 29, 2019, https://finance.yahoo.com/news/fidelity-creates-blockchain-token-reward-210032878.html.

Chapter 4. Security Tokens Will Massively Disrupt and Vastly Improve Markets

1. Melanie Curtin, "The Big Thing Blockchain Needs that No One's Talking About", Inc., September 15, 2018, https://www.inc.com/melanie-curtin/the-problem-with-blockchain-that-no-ones-talking-about.html.

2. BlockState. "Smart Asset Financing". Accessed April 1, 2020. https://blockstate.com/.

3. Alec Ziupsnys, "How $544 Trillion Worth of Assets Could Become Tokenized", The Tokenist, September 15, 2019, https://thetokenist.io/how-544-trillion-worth-of-assets-could-become-tokenized/.

4. Tim Moran, "Blockchain-based Mobile Payments Aim to Boost International Remittances", American Express, Accessed April 1, 2020, https://www.americanexpress.com/us/foreign-exchange/articles/blockchain-based-mobile-payments-boost-international-remittances/.

Chapter 6. The Security Token Ecosystem

1. Kepler Finance. "Digital Securities Market Research 2019 by Kepler Finance". Hacker Noon. February 4, 2019. https://hackernoon.com/digital-securities-market-research-2019-by-kepler-finance-aab927734f80.

Chapter 7. Regulation of Digital Assets

1. CoinSchedule. "Total Raised in the Period". Crypto Token Sales Market Statistics. Accessed April 1, 2020. https://www.coinschedule.com/stats.

2.   Abdelkrim Krid, "Prime Minister to Attend Malta Blockchain Summit", AIBC Summit Malta, August 23, 2018, https://maltablockchainsummit.com/news/prime-minister-to-attend-malta-blockchain-summit/.

3.   Katharina Bart, "Thomas Zeeb: 'We may Issue our own Tokens'", Finews, May 6, 2019, https://www.finews.com/news/english-news/36357-thomas-zeeb-itvu-e.

4.   Wayne Pisani, "Malta introduces New Regulations Governing Virtual Financial Assets", Grant Thornton, Accessed April 1, 2020, https://www.grantthornton.com.mt/industry/fintech-and-innovation/The-Malta-Virtual-Financial-Asset-Act/.

5.   Bermuda Laws Online. "Digital Asset Business Act of 2018". Bermuda Acts and Statutory Instruments. Accessed April 1, 2020, http://www.bermudalaws.bm/laws/Annual%20Laws/2018/Acts/Digital%20Asset%20Business%20Act%202018.pdf.

6.   GBX Digital Asset Exchange. "Our Story". GSX Group. Accessed April 1, 2020. https://www.gbx.global/our-story/.

7.   Aliya Allen, "GT ATTORNEYS REVIEW DARE BILL 2019", Grant Thompson, June 24, 2019, https://grahamthompson.com/updates/gt-attorneys-review-dare-bill-2019/.

8.   BNAmercas. "Bahamas Plans to Launch Digital Currency". News. June 25, 2018. https://www.bnamericas.com/en/news/bahamas-plans-to-launch-digital-currency.

9.   Credit Suisse Research Institution. "Credit Suisse Global Wealth Report, 2018". International Wealth Management. October 2018. https://www.credit-suisse.com/media/assets/corporate/docs/about-us/research/publications/global-wealth-databook-2018.pdf.

10. Shannon Liao, "US Regulators are Struggling to Rein in Illegal Cryptocurrency Offerings", The Verge, February 6, 2018, https://www.theverge.com/2018/2/6/16978636/bitcoin-cryptocurrency-virtual-us-regulation-securities-sec-cftc-congress.

11. Wikipedia. "SEC v. W. J. Howey Co.". Last modified November 5, 2019. https://en.wikipedia.org/wiki/SEC_v._W._J._Howey_Co.

12. CoinTelegraph. "What is Ripple. Everything You Need to Know". Accessed April 6, 2020. https://cointelegraph.com/ripple-101/what-is-ripple.

13. XRP Ledger. "XRP". Concepts. Accessed April 6, 2020. https://xrpl.org/xrp.html.

14. Ripple. "Our Customers". Accessed April 2, 2020. https://ripple.com/customers/.

15. Nikhilesh De, "SEC Guidance Gives Ammo to Lawsuit Claiming XRP Is Unregistered Security", CoinDesk, August 13, 2019, https://www.coindesk.com/investors-suing-ripple-cite-sec-guidance-to-argue-xrp-is-a-security.

16. Tim Fries, "UK Financial Conduct Authority (FCA) Does Not Consider Ripple's XRP to Be a Security", The Tokenist, September 15, 2019, https://thetokenist.io/uk-financial-conduct-authority-fca-does-not-consider-ripples-xrp-to-be-a-security/.

17. XRP Ledger. "XRP Ledger Overview". Concepts. Accessed April 1, 2020. https://xrpl.org/xrp-ledger-overview.html.

18. Lubomir Tassev, "Lawsuit Against Ripple May Decide the Fate of XRP but Regulators Have the Final Say", Bitcoin.com, January 20, 2020, https://news.bitcoin.com/lawsuit-against-ripple-may-decide-the-fate-of-xrp-but-regulators-have-the-final-say/.

19. Arnone & Sicomo, "Cryptocurrencies and Blockchain Law in Luxembourg: How to Make Safe Investments", Monday, February 24, 2020, https://www.mondaq.com/Technology/896676/Cryptocurrencies-and-Blockchain-Law-in-Luxembourg-How-to-Make-Safe-Investments.

20. Lubomir Tassev, "Estonia Issues Over 900 Licenses to Cryptocurrency Businesses", Bitcoin.com, November 17, 2018, https://news.bitcoin.com/estonia-issues-over-900-licenses-to-cryptocurrency-businesses/.

21. Andrea Bianconi, "The first STO milestone is German: Bitbond issues the first BaFin approved security token bond", Hackernoon, March 5, 2019, https://hackernoon.com/the-first-sto-milestone-is-german-bitbond-issues-the-first-bafin-approved-security-token-bond-70925e61f2d.

22. Matus Steis, "New Regulations in Europe planned for 2019 will simplify issuance of Security Tokens", Medium, January 3, 2019, https://medium.com/rockaway-blockchain/new-regulations-in-europe-planned-for-2019-will-simplify-issuance-of-security-tokens-d5e3f91c8387.

23. European Securities and Markets Authority. "National thresholds below which the obligation to publish a prospectus does not apply". Rules in the Prospectus Regulation. March 2, 2020. https://www.esma.europa.eu/sites/default/files/library/esma31-62-1193_prospectus_thresholds.pdf

24. Yessi Bello Perez, "UK financial watchdog finally decides which cryptocurrencies it wants to regulate", The Next Web, July 31, 2019, https://thenextweb

.com/hardfork/2019/07/31/uk-financial-watchdog-finally-decides-which-cryptocurrencies-it-wants-to-regulate/.

25. Zheping Huang and Olga Kharif, "Cryptocurrency exchanges across China halt services amid crackdown", Japan Times, November 28, 2019, https://www.japantimes.co.jp/news/2019/11/28/business/chinas-crackdown-cryptocurrencies-claims-first-victims/#.XnYG34hKg2w

26. Yuan Yang, "What is China's digital currency plan?", Financial Times, November 2019, https://www.ft.com/content/e3f9c3c2-0aaf-11ea-bb52-34c8d9dc6d84.

27. Darren Kleine, "Bitcoin Declared Legal Commodity In Chinese Court", Crypto Briefing, July 18, 2019, https://cryptobriefing.com/bitcoin-declared-legal-commodity-in-chinese-court/.

28. Nicole Jao, "Bank of China releases infographic to raise bitcoin awareness", TechNode, July 29, 2019, https://technode.com/2019/07/29/bank-of-china-infographic-bitcoin/.

29. Greenberg Traurig. "New Regulations in Japan on Security Token Offerings". Insights. July 24, 2019. https://www.gtlaw.com/en/insights/2019/7/new-regulations-in-japan-on-security-token-offerings.

30. Richard Meyer, "Six Major Japanese Brokerages Form Security Token Offering Association", CoinDesk, October 2, 2019, https://www.coindesk.com/six-major-japanese-brokerages-form-security-token-offering-association.

31. Biser Dimitrov, "Why China's Blockchain Plan is Winning and The U.S. Should Pay Attention", Forbes, November 25, 2019, https://www.forbes.com/sites/biserdimitrov/2019/11/25/why-china-blockchain-plan-is-winning-and-the-us-should-pay-attention/#545aa6925e7e.

32. Helen Partz, "Bahamas Central Bank Enters Agreement to Deliver First National Digital Currency by 2020", CoinTelegraph, May 29, 2019, https://cointelegraph.com/news/bahamas-central-bank-enters-agreement-to-deliver-first-national-digital-currency-by-2020.

33. David Paul, "Why the Marshall Islands Is Issuing Its Own Cryptocurrency", CoinDesk, September 4, 2019, https://www.coindesk.com/why-the-marshall-islands-is-issuing-its-own-cryptocurrency.

Chapter 8. Markets for Digital Assets & Security Tokens

1. Melvin Wong, "Difference Between ICO, IEO and STO", January 5, 2019, Kodorra, https://kodorra.com/difference-between-ico-ieo-and-sto/.

2. iSTOX. "About Us". Accessed March 29, 2020. https://istox.com/.

3. iSTOX. "Private Capital". Accessed March 29, 2020. https://istox.com/# private-capital.

4. JD Alois, "DLT-based Securities Platform iStox 'Graduates' From Monetary Authority of Singapore Fintech Sandbox, Now Fully Regulated to Offer & Trade Securities", Crowd Fund Insider, February 3, 2020, https://www .crowdfundinsider.com/2020/02/157065-dlt-based-securities-platform-istox- graduates-from-monetary-authority-of-singapore-fintech-sandbox-now-fully- regulated-to-offer-trade-securities/.

5. Wikipedia. "Alternative Trading System". Last modified April 4, 2018. https:// en.wikipedia.org/wiki/Alternative_trading_system.

6. US Securities and Exchange Commission. "SEC Adopts Rules to Enhance Transparency and Oversight of Alternative Trading Systems". Press Release. July 18, 2018. https://www.sec.gov/news/press-release/2018-136.

7. Nathan Krishnan S, "Equity Levels of Value: The Logic Behind Premiums and Discounts", Toptal, Accessed April 1, 2020, https://www.toptal.com/finance/ valuation/value-of-assets.

8. Jonathon Ford, "The exorbitant privilege enjoyed by private equity firms", FT, September 8, 2019, https://www.ft.com/content/e089cd78-d223-11e9-a0bd- ab8ec6435630.

9. Stuart Pinnington, "Blockchain and private equity: a marriage made in heaven?", Private Funds CFO, October 15, 2018, https://www.privatefundscfo .com/blockchain-private-equity-marriage-made-heaven/.

10. Gertrude Chavez-Dreyfuss, "Paxos to launch settlement of U.S.-listed equities after SEC's no-action letter", Reuters, October 28, 2019, https://www.reuters .com/article/us-crypto-currencies-paxos/paxos-to-launch-settlement-of-u-s- listed-equities-after-secs-no-action-letter-idUSKBN1X727M.

11. David Pimentel, "Securities and Exchange Board of India to Study Blockchain", Block Tribune, August 17, 2017, https://blocktribune.com/securities- exchange-board-india-study-blockchain/.

12. Parnika Sokhi, "India's biggest bourse steps closer to blockchain adoption", IBS Intelligence, Accessed April 1, 2020, https://ibsintelligence.com/ibs-journal/ ibs-news/nse-blockchain-poc/.

13. Yogita Khatri, "Deutsche Börse, Swisscom Team Up to Build Digital Asset 'Ecosystem'", CoinDesk, March 11, 2019, https://www.coindesk.com/ deutsche-borse-swisscom-team-up-to-build-digital-asset-ecosystem.

14. Carol Gaszcz, "Euronext invests €5M in blockchain fintech Tokeny Solutions", The Block, July 5, 2019, https://www.theblockcrypto.com/linked/30222/euronext-invests-e5m-in-blockchain-fintech-tokeny-solutions.

15. Oliver Hirt, "Swiss exchange SIX to launch blockchain bourse in second half", Reuters, February 6, 2019, https://www.reuters.com/article/us-six-blockchain/swiss-exchange-six-to-launch-blockchain-bourse-in-second-half-idUSKCN1PV2D2.

16. William Foxley, "Australian Securities Exchange Building New Blockchain Platform With VMWare, Digital Asset", CoinDesk, August 28, 2019, https://www.coindesk.com/australian-securities-exchange-building-new-blockchain-platform-with-vmware-digital-asset.

17. Nikhilesh De, "Bakkt to Launch Crypto 'Consumer App' in First Half of 2020", CoinDesk, October 28, 2019, https://www.coindesk.com/bakkt-to-launch-crypto-consumer-app-in-first-half-of-2020.

Chapter 9. "DeFi" - eLending and the Future of Getting a Loan

1. CoinMarketCap. "Top 100 Cryptocurrencies by Market Capitalization". Rankings. Accessed April 1, 2020. https://coinmarketcap.com/.

2. The Block. "Crypto Credit & Lending". Theblockcrypto.com. Accessed March 29, 2020. https://moonwhale.io/crypto-collateral-p2p-lending/.

3. Daniel Strauss, "Trump has ramped up calls for negative interest rates. Here's what they are and why they matter", Markets Insider, September 11, 2019, https://markets.businessinsider.com/news/stocks/negative-interest-rates-explained-what-they-are-why-they-matter-2019-8-1028516867.

4. Accenture. "Mortgage and Blockchain: Ready for Disruption?". Accenture Credit Services. Accessed April 1, 2020. https://www.mba.org/Documents/Member%20White%20Papers/Accenture%20-%20Mortgage%20and%20Blockchain%202019.04.23.pdf.

5. Home Loan Experts. "How A Blockchain Mortgage Works". Blockchain Mortgage. Accessed March 21, 2020. https://www.homeloanexperts.com.au/home-loan-articles/blockchain-mortgage/.

6. Kathleen Howley, "U.S. home values reach a record high of $26.1 trillion in Q1, Fed says", Housing Wire, June 6, 2019, https://www.housingwire.com/articles/49282-us-home-values-reach-a-record-high-of-261-trillion-in-q1-fed-says/.

7. Allen Taylor, "Go Figure: Putting HELOCs and Lease Backs on the Blockchain", Lending Times, October 9, 2018, https://lending-times.com/2018/10/09/go-figure-putting-helocs-and-lease-backs-on-the-blockchain/.

8. PYMNTS. "Figure's Mike Cagney on How Blockchain Is Reinventing Lending". Blockchain. December 10, 2019. https://www.pymnts.com/blockchain/2019/figures-mike-cagney-on-how-blockchain-is-reinventing-lending/.

9. Jessica Guerin, "Figure Technologies lands $1 billion blockchain investment to revolutionize HELOC lending", Housing Wire, May 9, 2019, https://www.housingwire.com/articles/49009-figure-technologies-lands-1-billion-blockchain-investment-to-revolutionize-heloc-lending/.

10. Wikipedia. "New Century". Accessed April 17, 2020. https://en.wikipedia.org/wiki/New_Century.

11. Wikipedia. "Subprime mortgage crisis". Accessed April 17, 2020. https://en.wikipedia.org/wiki/Subprime_mortgage_crisis.

12. John Dunbar and David Donald, "Roots of the Financial Crisis: Who's to Blame", Public Integrity, May 19, 2014, https://publicintegrity.org/inequality-poverty-opportunity/the-roots-of-the-financial-crisis-who-is-to-blame/.

Chapter 10. Digital Adoption

1. Marc Andreesen, "Why Bitcoin Matters", New York Times, January 21, 2014, https://dealbook.nytimes.com/2014/01/21/why-bitcoin-matters/?mtrref=www.google.com&gwh=E0634FD774C2AA3FE1D1BDB0B4E63CBE&gwt=pay&assetType=REGIWALL.

2. ING Group. "Cracking the Code on Cryptocurrency". ING International Survey Mobile Banking – Cryptocurrency. June 2018. https://think.ing.com/uploads/reports/ING_International_Survey_Mobile_Banking_2018.pdf.

3. Blockchain.info. "Blockchain Wallet Users". Blockchain Charts. Accessed March 21, 2020. https://www.blockchain.com/charts.

4. Grayscale Investments and Q8 Research. "Bitcoin: 2019 Investor Study". July 2019. https://dropgold.com/bitcoin-investor-report/?utm_medium=pr&utm_source=release&utm_campaign=2019_q3_BTC_in_sur

5. Marissa Arnold, "Grayscale Investments Study Reveals More Than a Third of U.S. Investors Are Interested in Bitcoin", Globe Newswire, July 25, 2019, https://www.globenewswire.com/news-release/2019/07/25/1888060/0/en/Grayscale-Investments-Study-Reveals-More-Than-a-Third-of-U-S-Investors-Are-Interested-in-Bitcoin.html

6. Yogita Khatri, "Grayscale survey: More than one-third of American investors would consider buying bitcoin", The Block, July 25, 2019, https://www.theblockcrypto.com/post/33406/grayscale-survey-70-of-bitcoin-interested-investors-in-us-are-parents.

7. Wikipedia. "Internet". Last modified March 11, 2020. https://en.wikipedia.org/wiki/Internet.

8. Wikipedia. "Domain Name System". Last modified March 8, 2020. https://en.wikipedia.org/wiki/Domain_Name_System.

9. Chris McCann, "12 Graphs That Show Just How Early The Cryptocurrency Market Is", Medium, May 7, 2018, https://medium.com/@mccannatron/12-graphs-that-show-just-how-early-the-cryptocurrency-market-is-653a4b8b2720.

10. Statista. "Number of Blockchain wallet users worldwide from 3rd quarter 2016 to 4th quarter 2019". Financial Markets. Accessed April 1, 2020. https://www.statista.com/statistics/647374/worldwide-blockchain-wallet-users/.

11. FIO Foundation. Homepage. Accessed April 6, 2020. https://fio.foundation/.

12. YPULSE, "Millennial Banking Update: Losing Patience, Spending Less, & Going Mobile". Finance. July 28, 2016. https://evenfinancial.com/blog/facebook-report-exposes-millennials-financial-frustrations/.

13. Even Financial. "Facebook Report Exposes Millennials' Financial Frustrations". Blog. https://evenfinancial.com/blog/facebook-report-exposes-millennials-financial-frustrations/

14. Zach Conway, "Why More Millennials Would Rather Visit The Dentist Than Listen To Banks", Forbes, April 19, 2017, https://www.forbes.com/sites/zachconway/2017/04/19/why-more-millennials-would-rather-visit-the-dentist-than-listen-to-banks/#1829cdc872b3.

15. Greenwich. "Security Tokens: Cryptonite for Stock Certificates". June 6, 2019. https://www.greenwich.com/market-structure-technology/security-tokens-cryptonite-stock-certificates.

16. Billy Bambrough, "Could Google Be About To Break Bitcoin?", Forbes, October 2, 2019, https://www.forbes.com/sites/billybambrough/2019/10/02/could-google-be-about-to-break-bitcoin/#7ee091a43329.

17. Kate Rooney, "Electronic payments look more appealing as people fear cash could spread coronavirus", CNBC, March 16, 2020, https://www.cnbc.com/2020/03/16/electronic-payments-look-more-appealing-as-coronavirus-spreads.html.

18. Melissa Luz Lopez, "Stock market to reopen Thursday after 2-day shutdown due to COVID-19", CNN Philippines, March 18, 2020, https://cnnphilippines .com/business/2020/3/18/Stock-market-reopening-March-19.html.

19. The Depository Trust Company. "Important Notice". March 26, 2020. https:// www.dtcc.com/-/media/Files/pdf/2020/3/26/13154-20.pdf.

20. Daphne Foreman, "Banking and Cash During COVID-19 Crisis: Some Branches Close, Yet ATM Fees May be Waived", Forbes, March 30, 2020, https://www.forbes.com/sites/advisor/2020/03/19/banking-and-cash-during-covid-19-crisis-some-branches-close-atm-fees-may-be-waived/# 4f72ac4d1c6d.

21. Heather Long and Michelle Singletary, "Glitches prevent $1,200 stimulus checks from reaching millions of Americans", Washington Post, April 16, 2020, https://www.washingtonpost.com/business/2020/04/16/coronavirus-cares-stimulus-check/.

22. Nilkhilesh De and Zack Seward, "US Senate Floats 'Digital Dollar' Bill After House Scrubs Term from Coronavirus Relief Plan" , Coin Desk, March 24, 2020, https://www.coindesk.com/us-senate-floats-digital-dollar-bill-after-house-scrubs-term-from-coronavirus-relief-plan.

23. Samuel Stolton, "LEAK: EU in Push for Digital Transformation after COVID-19 Crisis", Euractiv, April 6, 2020, https://www.euractiv.com/ section/digital/news/leak-eu-in-push-for-digital-transformation-after-covid-19-crisis/.

24. Danny Nelson, "Researchers at the Bank for International Settlements (BIS) think COVID-19 may Accelerate the Adoption of Digital Payments and Sharpen the Debate over Central Bank Digital Currencies (CBDC)", CoinDesk, April 3, 2020, https://www.coindesk.com/bis-researchers-say-coronavirus-could-spur-central-banks-to-adopt-digital-payments.

25. Ledger Insights. "UAE uses Blockchain, Digital Identity to Battle Covid-19". Accessed April 16, 2020. https://www.ledgerinsights.com/uae-uses-blockchain-digital-identity-to-battle-covid-19/.

26. Le Shen, "Alipay Announces Three-Year Plan to Support the Digital Trans-formation of 40 Million Service Providers in China", March 10, 2020, Business Wire, https://www.businesswire.com/news/home/20200309005906/ en/Alipay-Announces-Three-Year-Plan-Support-Digital-Transformation.

27. Coin Market Cap. Currencies - Bitcoin. Accessed April 16, 2020. https:// coinmarketcap.com/currencies/bitcoin/.

28. Coin Market Cap. Currencies - Ethereum. Accessed April 16, 2020. https://coinmarketcap.com/currencies/ethereum/.

29. Yahoo. Finance. Accessed April 16, 2020. https://finance.yahoo.com/quote/ACWI/.

30. Coin Market Cap. Currencies – USDCoin. Accessed April 16, 2020. https://coinmarketcap.com/currencies/usd-coin/.

31. Coin Market Cap. Currencies - Tether. Accessed April 16, 2020. https://coinmarketcap.com/currencies/tether/.

32. Catherine Muccigrosso, "Charlotte grocery store update: Temperature checks, customer caps and contactless pay", Charlotte Observer, April 6, 2020, https://www.charlotteobserver.com/news/business/biz-columns-blogs/whats-in-store/article241714656.html.

33. Joshua Stoner, "The COVID-19 Effect", Securities.io, March 24, 2020, https://www.securities.io/the-covid-19-effect/.

34. Paxos. Careers. Accessed April 16, 2020. https://www.paxos.com/careers/.

35. Indeed. Find Jobs. Accessed April 16, 2020. https://www.indeed.com/q-Crypto-l-Jersey-City,-NJ-jobs.html.

Concluding Thoughts

1. Shintya Felicitas, "Mobile payments: Asia leading the world", Asia Fund Managers, August 12, 2019, https://www.asiafundmanagers.com/int/mobile-payments/.

2. Hagen Rooke, "Rise and Rise of Mobile Payments in Asia", The Garage, May 23, 2019, https://www.businesstimes.com.sg/garage/rise-and-rise-of-mobile-payments-in-asia.

3. Phuong Nguyen, "Southeast Asia's mobile payments face shakeout as market booms", Reuters, October 16, 2019, https://www.reuters.com/article/us-southeastasia-payments-analysis/southeast-asias-mobile-payments-face-shakeout-as-market-booms-idUSKBN1WV2V7.

4. Eileen Yu, "Asia Driving Global Mobile Payments, with Eight in Top 10 Markets", ZDNet, April 12, 2019, https://www.zdnet.com/article/asia-driving-global-mobile-payments-with-eight-in-top-10-markets/.

5. PwC. "PwC Global Consumer Insights Survey". 2019. https://www.pwc.com/gx/en/consumer-markets/consumer-insights-survey/2019/report.pdf.

6. Yogita Khatri, "Chinese Tech Giants Tencent, Alibaba Filed for The Most Blockchain Patents Last Year", The Block Crypto, April 12, 2020, https://www .theblockcrypto.com/linked/61547/chinese-tech-giants-tencent-alibaba-filed-for-the-most-blockchain-patents-last-year.

7. Stella Yifan Xie, "More Than a Third of China Is Now Invested in One Giant Mutual Fund", Wall Street Journal, arch 27, 2019, https://www.wsj.com/ articles/more-than-a-third-of-china-is-now-invested-in-one-giant-mutual-fund-11553682785.

8. Wikipedia. "Ant Financial". Last modified February 22, 2020. https://en .wikipedia.org/wiki/Ant_Financial.

9. Asia Money. "Ant Financial: How a Bug Took on the World". Euro Money. September 26, 2019. https://www.euromoney.com/article/b1h7mtyfd5d8lg/ ant-financial-how-a-bug-took-on-the-world.

10. Le Shen, "Alipay Announces Three-Year Plan to Support the Digital Transformation of 40 Million Service Providers in China", Business Wire, March 10, 2020, https://www.businesswire.com/news/home/20200309005906/en/ Alipay-Announces-Three-Year-Plan-Support-Digital-Transformation.

11. Marie Huillet, "Ant Financial Aims to Launch Its Enterprise Blockchain Platform This Month", Coin Telegraph, January 8, 2020, https://cointelegraph .com/news/ant-financial-aims-to-launch-its-enterprise-blockchain-platform-this-month

12. "Pirates of Silicon Valley", directed by Martyn Burke, featuring Anthony Michael Hall and Noah Wyle (Haft Entertainment, 1999), https://www.imdb .com/title/tt000168122/quotes/?tab=qt&ref_=tt_trv_qu.

13. Wikipedia. "MySpace". Last modified April 17, 2020. https://en.wikipedia.org/ wiki/Ant_Financial.

14. Frances Coppola, "Tether's U.S. Dollar Peg Is No Longer Credible", Forbes, March 14, 2019, https://www.forbes.com/sites/francescoppola/2019/03/14/ tethers-u-s-dollar-peg-is-no-longer-credible/#dd8f648451be.

15. CoinMarketCap. "Tether Charts". Charts. Accessed April 1, 2020. https:// coinmarketcap.com/currencies/tether/.

16. CoinMarketCap. "Top 100 Cryptocurrencies by Market Capitalization". Rankings. Accessed April 1, 2020. https://coinmarketcap.com/.

17. CoinTelegraph. "What Is Lightning Network and How It Works". Accessed March 21, 2020. https://cointelegraph.com/lightning-network-101/what-is-lightning-network-and-how-it-works.

18. Rakesh Sharmak, "Seychelles National Stock Exchange Offers Tokenized Shares in its IPO", September 12, 2019. https://coinnotes.news/2019/09/12/seychelles-national-stock-exchange-offers-tokenized-shares-in-its-ipo/.

19. Wikipedia. "AOL". Last modified March 18, 2020. https://en.wikipedia.org/wiki/AOL.

20. Wikipedia. "Netscape". Last modified February 27, 2020. https://en.wikipedia.org/wiki/Netscape.

21. Alex Planes, "The IPO That Inflated the Dot-Com Bubble", Motley Fool, August 9, 2013, https://www.fool.com/investing/general/2013/08/09/the-ipo-that-inflated-the-dot-com-bubble.aspx.

22. Wikipedia. "Browser Wars". Last modified February 24, 2020. https://en.wikipedia.org/wiki/Browser_wars#First_Browser_War:_1995-2001.

23. Wikipedia. "Yahoo!". Last modified February 20, 2020. https://en.wikipedia.org/wiki/Yahoo!.

24. Mike Murphy, "Yahoo's Share Price Since its IPO in 1996", The Atlas, Accessed April 8, 2020, https://theatlas.com/charts/B1RjK9Q_.

25. Wikipedia. "Web Search Engine". Last modified March 19, 2020. https://en.wikipedia.org/wiki/Web_search_engine#Market_share.

ADDITIONAL RESOURCES

Sites for Digital Asset News:

1. cointelegraph.com
2. coindesk.com
3. cryptonews.com
4. bitcoinist.com
5. thetokenist.io
6. securities.io
7. decrypt.co
8. totalcrypto.io
9. cryptovest.com
10. tokenmarket.net

Podcasts and YouTube Media:

1. <u>Security Token Academy with Adam Chapnick</u> – Great source that aggregates news, insights and information about security tokens and security token offerings. The Security Token Academy provides online video content and live events that feature interviews with industry experts, blockchain project reviews and regulatory analysis.

   The organization's website has rich content on its "Security Token Edge," "The Digital Wrapper," and "Security Token Stories" segments.

2. <u>Off the Chain with Anthony Pompliano</u> – This popular podcast includes content discussing how both old and new players in the financial markets are thinking about digital assets. The show offers insights from a wide array of perspectives and goes over many facets of how blockchain is disrupting the world of finance.

   Host Anthony Pompliano, simply referred to as "Pomp," frequently interviews guests who are some of the most respected names on Wall Street. His discussions typically center around blockchain adoption, risks and benefits.

3. <u>DataDash with Nicolas Merten</u> – Likely the largest YouTube channel covering cryptocurrencies. Discussions revolve around all things crypto with a bent toward science and data analytics.

The host, Nicholas Merton, is well respected as a crypto-analyst and routinely provides thought leadership at major international blockchain conferences.

4. BnkToTheFuture with Simon Dixon – As early adopters of crypto, BnkToThe-Future has long been on the leading edge of digitization. The firm facilitates investment in blockchain and FinTech companies. The group holds a strong belief that the future of finance will be strongly shaped by blockchain and that new and innovative products will be developed using the technology. Host Simon Dixon streams live content on roughly a weekly basis.

5. Security Token Show with Kyle Sonlin & Herwig Konings – This weekly show is the first of its kind directly focusing on security tokens. Entrepreneurs Kyle and Herwig dedicate each segment to one particular topic of tokenization while also highlighting their "Projects of the Week" and the latest news and trends in digitization.

6. Bitcoin Radio with Joe Blackburn and Amanda Schmidgall – These podcasts review the latest news and hot topics in crypto. Segments provide laid-back, enjoyable discussions and colorful interviews with guests.

7. Coin Bureau with Guy "The Crypto Guy" – This YouTube channel features deep-dive segments that discuss new projects, exchanges and trends in the digital space. Shows exhibit well-researched content and high production quality.

Leading Organizations on Blockchain and Digital Finance:

1. The Blockchain Center of Excellence in Sam M. Walton College of Business at The University of Arkansas – Established in 2018 with the vision to make the Walton College a premiere academic leader of blockchain application research and education. The BCoE is led by Dr. Mary C. Lacity and works with major Arkansas-based companies in its blockchain curricula and research including the world's largest retailer, Wal-Mart.
   blockchain.uark.edu

2. Blockchain Research Institute – This Toronto-based think-tank consults orga-nizations on how to best position themselves to fully capture the benefits of the blockchain revolution. Founders Don and Alex Tapscott are world-renown speakers and best selling authors. The group's community includes over 60 mem-ber institutions from government agencies to academic researchers to Fortune 500 corporations.
   blockchainresearchinstitute.org

3. Blockchain at UCLA – This university student-run community aims to foster networking, research and education throughout the field of blockchain. The initiative develops opportunities through campus events and community engage-ments.
   blockchainatucla.com

4. <u>Dusk Network</u> – This group aims to tackle the challenges of solving privacy, scalability and compliance in blockchain solutions. One objective of the group is to create smart contracts for digital assets and securities.
    dusk.network

5. <u>Cambridge Research Hub</u> – UK-based think-tank committed to the development of blockchain policy. The Cambridge Research Forum is design to be a hub for blockchain learning which brings together persons from government, industry and academia.
    cambridgeblockchain.org

Cryptocurrency Exchanges:

1. Coinbase – coinbase.com
2. Binance – binance.com
3. Kraken – kraken.com
4. Huobi – huobi.com
5. Poloniex – poloniex.com
6. Gemini – gemini.com
7. Etoro – etoro.com

Decentralized Finance, or DeFi, Offerings:

1. Celsius – celsius.network
2. Nexo – nexo.io
3. BlockFi – blockfi.com
4. SALT – saltlending.com
5. dYDx – dYdX.exchange
6. Compound Finance – compound.finance
7. Figure Technologies – figure.com
8. Home Loan Experts – homeloanexperts.com.au

ABOUT THE AUTHOR

Baxter Hines, CFA, is managing partner with Honeycomb Digital Investments. He co-founded the firm in 2020 to provide income producing solutions for clients. His firm manages portfolios consisting of traditional assets, security tokens, and digital assets.

Mr. Hines was a managing director, portfolio manager, and co-lead for several internationally focused value strategies during his 12 years with NFJ Investment Group, a wholly owned subsidiary of Allianz Global Investors. Prior to his time with NFJ, he was an analyst with the Teacher Retirement Systems of Texas and worked as financial systems specialist for Reuters. He holds a bachelor's degree in economics from the University of Virginia and an MBA in finance from the University of Texas. His investment philosophy and market outlook have been profiled in several financial publications, including *Barron's* and the *Wall Street Journal*. Mr. Hines holds the Chartered Financial Analyst designation and is a member of the CFA Society of Dallas.

Mr. Hines is a current board member and former chairman of Camp Summit, a Dallas-based charity providing summer camp experiences to persons with disabilities. He lives with his wife and two children in Dallas, Texas.

INDEX